ALL IN

A MARRIAGE WORTH DYING FOR

Rob Thorpe

First published by All In Marriage, Inc. 09/01/2015

ISBN: 978-0-9833205-8-6 - paperback
ISBN: 978-0-9833205-7-9 - ebook

Printed in the United States of America

For more information, contact:

All In Marriage at marriagesthatmatter@gmail.com

Find additional resources on our website - allinmarriage.org

Follow Rob on Twitter at - twitter.com/husbandmentor

Follow All In Marriage at - Facebook.com/allinformarriage

Contact Rob or the Ministry at: marriagesthatmatter@gmail.com

Certain stock imagery © iStockphoto, Bigstockphoto and Clipart.com

Design by Tony Barmann

Because of the dynamic nature of the Internet, any web addresses or links contained in this book may have changed since publication and may no longer be valid.

ALL IN

A MARRIAGE WORTH DYING FOR

Rob Thorpe

Contents

Forward

In our culture, we are destroying the idea of marriage. It's not just those who aren't Christian and those who don't go to church, it's all of the above. Christian and non-Christian alike!

With stats of around 50%, marriages are failing with those who believe in Jesus and those who don't. The culture is more likely to live together than get married and the trend doesn't seem to be stopping anytime soon. We are on a brutal course of destroying the biblical idea of marriage and family if something doesn't happen soon!

Our churches, government, and society have all walked away from the word of God. And its starting to show!

I have always said "that if a book doesn't take you back to THE book (the Bible) then put it down". Rob's book, All In, does exactly that! Every chapter is filled with scripture and references to seek out what God says! It doesn't matter what I say or what Rob says, but it matters what God says. All In gives you all that and much more.

All In is not just another book about marriage. But it's a book that shows you how marriage was meant to be and how it can be again if we will only follow God's plan and not the worlds! Rob's years of experience in marriage ministry show up throughout the book and his insight is perfectly meshed with the topic and scripture provided.

My prayer is that this book heals every person and marriage that reads it! I can tell you, it has helped my marriage!

Jody Burkeen

Founder, Man Up God's Way and author of Man Up - Becoming a Godly Man in an Ungodly World.

Introduction

You will find very quickly that this book is not intended to remind you of relationship principles to follow (which you most probably already know). It is not filled with new and helpful relationship tips you can attempt to practice in order to stay in your spouse's good graces.

I pray this is a different book, a book about the heart of God and His heart for marriage - your marriage. You don't need more marriage information. We have more information today than ever before in history and marriages are still falling apart all around us. Information is wonderful and necessary - but information alone will not produce transformation.

You cannot learn your way to an extraordinary marriage.

My prayer is that God will use this book to captivate your heart to the point where you will allow Him to transform it, and by doing so, transform your marriage. I pray that you will see God's love for you and His design for your marriage in a whole new light.

Ask God to speak to you here. Don't read this just to get to the end. Read it with your heart and ears open to what God may speak to you personally.

This book, like any book on marriage, will not change a thing - if you are not personally committed to living intentionally each and every day of your life. If you and I will simply "do" what we know God requires of us - our lives and marriages will flourish.

So, thank you for reading the book. I am humbled. If it stirs your heart in any way, I pray that it stirs your heart to want to know

Christ more intimately, more deeply, more personally. I pray you will keep on asking Him to do for you what you cannot do by yourself ... die.

Only then can He live and love through you. Then you will experience the marriage you have longed for and see His love, wisdom and power manifest in your life like never before.

Rob

Chapter One
The Great Marriage

The first twenty-five verses of the Bible tell an amazing story of
Almighty God creating something astounding. Out of nothing,
out of darkness, God spoke - and the universe came to be. At
His word, "heavens, earth, land, water, light, day, night, oceans,
skies, vegetation, plants and trees, sun and moon, every living
creature on land and sea, wildlife, livestock, birds, insects,
amphibians, reptiles and mammals - everything on earth
and in the universe around it, farther than our most powerful
telescopes can see, was spoken into being by the voice of God.
Then, as an exclamation point, the last phrase is added -
"And God saw that it was good".

God was pleased. He rejoiced in what He had made. It was
splendid. It was spectacular. It was amazing.

But what happens next is the most amazing thing of all. You see,
everything God had just spoken into existence was created for
a purpose. From the very first word, God had an amazing and
wonderful plan in mind ... man.

But man (mankind) would need a place, a world, an environment, a home in which to dwell. Most parents take great care and go to great lengths to prepare a place, a home, and environment for their newborn children. They spend, decorate, coordinate, paint, build and hang. Everything must be in it's place when he/she arrives.

How utterly amazing - God created all of Genesis 1: 1-25 as a dwelling place for man. Man was not simply the next creation in a long line of created things. Man was the focal point. Man was the reason for everything being created in the first place. It was all for him to enjoy. It is all for us (you and me) to enjoy.

It is God's heart that when we gaze at the star-filled night sky, or enjoy a spectacular sunset, or gasp at the Grand Canyon - that we are filled with awe and wonder at the love and creativity of our Father. He placed those here for us. They are signposts intended to remind us of His great love for us and draw us back to Him.

Don't let that thought slip away. Don't just read the words. I hope you are at the point in your relationship with God that you can look at a sunset or a breathtaking Fall mountainside and hear Him speak to you, personally - "This is for you". I fear most of us are far too busy and too easily distracted by technology and busyness to hear Him shouting to us from His amazing creation all around us - every day ...

"You are special. You are loved. I created you on purpose and for a purpose. Your life was never intended to be lived apart from me."

So, into this amazing, new environment (earth) God does something very unique; something He hadn't done before. Genesis 1: 26-27 tells us that God next created man and woman, but it is Genesis 2:7 that gives us a peek into His heart.

Up until then God had created galaxies, stars, planets, light and darkness and a world filled with millions of living creatures - all by simply speaking. Everything came into being - just because God said so.

But not man; not you and me.

You see, we were made to enjoy a personal relationship with our Creator. Man alone was created "in God's image" in order to have the capacity to walk in communion with God and enjoy what no other created thing can. Take a moment to ponder God's own description of how man came to be in Chapter 2, verse 7:

> "Then the Lord God formed the man out of the dust from the ground and breathed the breath of life into his nostrils, and the man became a living being".

Here is the image that is fixed in my mind when I camp on this verse, and I long for you to grasp - A loving Father personally "forms" (molds/fashions) man with His own hands out of the dirt He had just created from nothing. He could have simply spoken man into existence, but He took the time to deliberately, purposefully and lovingly form him like a potter forms a priceless work of art. This shouts to me that God was very intentional about creating value in man and in establishing a relationship with man from the very first handful of dirt.

Then something even more amazing happens. After taking the time and the care to fashion this altogether unique creature - God once again does something He had never done before in all creation. He kneels down (my thoughts) and places His mouth over man's nostrils ... and breathes. He breathes His holy, loving, life-giving breath into this lifeless mannikin made of mud.

Miracles of heavenly proportion then occurred. That breath began to change dirt into bones, skin, organs, systems, blood, DNA, brain cells, nerve cells, etc ... .. Unbelievable! Billions of stars and galaxies are chicken feed compared to this.

Man becomes "a living soul/being". God's breath changed the dirt-man into a living soul, made in His very image. The last verse of Genesis 1 says that God then stepped back, looked at what He had created and said "this is very good". Creating man was the icing on the cake, the crowning achievement of the entire creation.

But wait ... there's more.

God is so smart. His ways are truly not our ways and His thoughts are not our thoughts (Isa.55:8). He created man first, and for good reason. If you read Genesis 2 too quickly you will miss it completely.

The Pre-Marital Counseling

You already know about the Garden of Eden, right? We all have heard about the Garden. It has been only recently that I realized why the Garden was so significant to man and also to marriage.

Genesis 2:8-17 tells the story of God planting an amazing Garden and filling it with a bounty of plants and trees. We are told that God "placed the man" in the Garden to "take care of" "work, tend" it.

Have you ever thought about that? Why did God create man and then "place him" or take him to a Garden to work? Why not place him at the beach under an umbrella - or just allow him to roam the magnificent countryside and enjoy creation?

One obvious answer is that man was created to work. Man, like God, was not created to be passive or idle. We are created to produce, create and yes - work. Not so obvious is the lesson that God is the One who "caused to grow out of the ground" all the bountiful crops He had planted. Man was intended simply to partner with God in that work, and to do his work "as unto the Lord" (Col. 3:23) - in other words, for His glory.

Work, as we know it today, was not work then. "Tending" had an altogether different meaning and connotation. Adam was to "steward" – to prune, to harvest, to keep the place clean and productive. He wasn't swinging a pic and driving a plow mule under the hot summer sun. Work was created to be enjoyable, satisfying and fruitful.

The Garden was the place where God (Jesus) would walk and talk with Adam every day. It was here that Adam enjoyed a daily fellowship with Jesus like no human has since. They talked, they dreamed, they planned, they laughed and they simply enjoyed each other's company. We are all created to walk with God like this and to have Him involved in every aspect of our daily lives.

———————————————

Can you really imagine a life like this? A day like this? Has the enemy (Satan) stolen from your heart the very idea that a life of daily fellowship and communion with Jesus is even possible? Has he convinced you that you are not worthy of that kind of life, or that God is mad at you for your past sins? He will try diligently to make you believe that you are "damaged goods" and that God doesn't hang out with people like you.

First, let me emphatically say - the "father of lies" (Satan) has been lying to you and desperately wants to keep you from discovering the truth that God still loves you, that He likes you, and that He wants to walk with you just like He did Adam.

Secondly, let me ask you to keep reading and, as you do, pray that God will reveal more of His heart and plan for your life and your marriage.

Now – back to Genesis ...

It was also here (Eden) that Adam was given specific instructions by God regarding a very important rule (commandment) that was to be followed or there would be dire consequences. God created man and gave him the right and the ability to think for himself, to make his own choices. God's love had to allow man to choose whether or not to love Him in return. One way man would show his love was by obeying the Creator's rules. More in Chapter 2.

So the Garden was Adam's training facility. He learned to work, but most importantly he learned about God, about life, about God's heart and His plans for the future. He marveled at God's creation and soaked up His wisdom. He learned about love - and experienced it firsthand - every day.

But, there was something else going on in that Garden. An education of a different kind. God loves us and He knows what we need. He knows what is ahead for us and what the next chapter of our lives will be. He knew there would be an Eve in the not-to-distant future and He took the opportunity to teach Adam some significant life lessons while there was just the two of them.

The Bible uses the Hebrew word to "tend" in speaking of Adam's role as gardener of Eden. Other significant interpretations of this word include: "to serve", "to care for", "to steward", "to watch over" and my personal favorite - "to husband".

God placed Adam in a delightful Garden that He had created - to learn to care for, steward, protect, serve, watch over and husband it. Knowing that Adam would soon have the divine opportunity and responsibility to "tend, serve, care for, steward, watch over and "husband" a different kind of "garden", a much more significant creation - called Eve.

In His great wisdom, God used this Garden environment to train Adam how to be a husband to the woman He would soon create and bring to him. What better way to watch over, encourage, train and mentor the young man who would become her husband.

The Longing

It has always fascinated me that God already knew that *"it is not good for man to be alone"*, when He created Adam. So why, after discussing with Adam his need for companionship, did God create all the living creatures and bring them to Adam to name? Why not simply create Eve immediately?

While my conclusion is not specifically explained in Scripture, I think it is valid based on my years as a man and a long time marriage mentor and counselor. I think God, in His wisdom, wanted Adam to have a season of time to develop a deep longing for his "counterpart" and to more deeply appreciate her (and God) when she finally arrived. Again - another huge lesson for the husband-to-be.

I find it interesting that Adam enjoyed the most intimate relationship with God that a human has ever enjoyed and yet God knew there were needs in Adam's life that could only be filled by another human being. He created Adam that way and He created us that way. We are created with a soul need for fellowship with our Creator and also with our counterpart, our "rest of me", our companion - our spouse.

God initiated the task of finding a "suitable" companion for Adam. He obviously could have created Eve immediately but chose another, less direct route. He created animals - hundreds and thousands and millions of animals - and brought them to Adam to see what he would name them. (Genesis 2:19-20).

[19] Now the Lord God had formed out of the ground all the wild animals and all the birds in the sky. He brought them to the man to see what he would name them; and whatever the man called each living creature, that was its name. [20] So the man gave names to all the livestock, the birds in the sky and all the wild animals.

According to Science Daily, there are somewhere between 7-9 million species of animals on the earth. If Adam saw one pair of each species every two minutes, with no bathroom or sleep breaks - he could name 720 a day. To name 8 million would take 111,111 days or over 30 years.

My guess is, God used His creative genius to help Adam out somehow. But, I am convinced it took Adam a very long time to name all the animals. Weeks, months, years? I don't know, but one thing I do know - during that extended timeframe, Adam saw male animals and female animals doing what male and female animals do. He no doubt noticed that every animal had a mate, a counterpart, a companion. He must have noticed affection, caring and couldn't have helped but notice intimate animal encounters.

By God's design, this evoked feelings and longings in Adam that he had never felt before. For the first time in his existence he felt lonely, needy, incomplete. **"But for Adam, there was not found a helper suitable for him",** according to Genesis 2:20. There was no counterpart, no companion, no one like him ... no one for him.

I'm sure he voiced his feelings and needs to his best friend - God. And in His perfect timing, God once again did what only He could do.

The Wedding

I find it quite wonderful that God could have created anything He wanted to create, out of anything He wanted to create it from, but God is an amazing and wise Creator/Father. I think He discussed with Adam the operation He was about to perform and Adam gladly volunteered to be put to sleep - trusting God's love and His plans for him.

While Adam slept, God took one of his ribs and "fashioned" it into what He considered the perfect solution to Adam's created need for companionship, intimacy and fulfillment. He didn't fashion it into a loyal labrador retriever, a new set of Ping golf clubs, a great paying new job, or a new Ford F-150 pickup - or even another male best buddy.

When he woke, Adam looked around and didn't see his surgeon (God) anywhere, and I'm sure wondered exactly what had just happened to him. Little did he know he was about to receive the gift of a lifetime.

God once again took the time to "fashion" (mold, shape, form) another human being, but this time by using a rib bone instead of dirt. Equally amazing, He took Adam's genetic material, then somehow molded a beautiful and perfectly complimentary human being of different gender and again breathed His life into her lungs. His breath once again caused organs, skin, systems, nerves, etc. to form and function perfectly.

God knew exactly what Adam needed, and in His divine wisdom created the perfect "helper, suitable for him" ... woman.

And - not just any woman. I am convinced also that the God who created galaxies, stars, planets, the Alps, sunsets, oceans, beaches, majestic animals and breathtaking landscapes - handmade a woman unequalled in beauty for all time. She was His handcrafted creation and based on His track record, I'd bet He did an amazing job.

So, back to poor, post-operative Adam.

As he awakens and is getting his bearings, he hears the sound of people talking as they are no doubt getting closer. But he has never heard one of the voices. This is an unfamiliar sound, but a pleasing, exciting one. His heart begins to beat faster and harder as they approach.

Genesis 2:22 says that God (as Jesus) "brought her to the man". This was a very epic moment in time. A truly historic occasion. Picture with me a wedding, set in the most beautiful Garden environment you can imagine. Perfect weather, perfect decor (flowers/foliage) and perfect timing. The anticipation could not have been stronger. Then, from around a grove of fruit trees appears Jesus arm in arm with the most beautiful and captivating creature Adam's eyes had ever seen (and he had seen them all).

There was no beautiful, white wedding gown but I am sure what she was "wearing" was altogether mind blowing. Another compliment to the Creator (and gift for Adam), I believe Eve was perfect physically as well as emotionally and spiritually. And besides, "naked" didn't mean anything to them since clothes weren't invented until the next Chapter. Adam was also wearing his birthday suit - but no one cared. I suppose all the wedding guests were naked too.

The Bible doesn't tell us all about the wedding that took place in that moment, in that perfect setting. But, just three verses later God speaks of Adam and Eve as husband and wife. This was not the first man and woman simply hooking up. This was designed by the Creator as the divine template for human relationships for all time. Marriage is God's primary blueprint for human companionship and fulfillment. It is His idea and He knows exactly what it takes to make it amazing. He doesn't create anything that is not beautiful, amazing and completely fulfilling.

Adam took one look at this uniquely beautiful creature - and shouted, "WOW", "This is what I have been waiting for... longing for! This is the rest of me, my other half, my compliment!!" (Genesis 2:23). He knew she was like him, actually part of him because God took his rib to fashion her. She, like no other creature on earth - was God's perfect gift to him alone. She was special. A meticulously designed masterpiece, given to him by his loving Father to enjoy for a lifetime.

> [24] For this reason a man will leave his father
> and his mother, and will be joined to his wife.
> And they will become one flesh.

God then adds verse 24, as an admonition to all those who were to follow Adam and Eve (since they had no earthly father and mother). What God had just divinely designed; what He had purposefully brought together and united in marriage - and the accompanying joy and fulfillment He intended for man and woman to experience would require them to leave their family of origin physically, emotionally, financially, etc. in order to experience.

Without the leaving, there will be no true cleaving. You can't be "glued together" as one flesh if your heart still runs back to your family for security, support, direction and approval.

"In my experience, 90% of marital discord can be traced back to a failure to leave" Dr. Dan Allender, Intimate Allies.

So the great wedding has taken place. God the Father brings His daughter to the man and performs the first ceremony, witnessed by a Garden full of animals and a sky full of angels. What a glorious sight indeed! A solemn, majestic, historic occasion.

Everything God had spoken into existence was to serve as a backdrop, a stage from which mankind would proclaim the glory of Almighty God in a "one flesh", marriage relationship. Created in His very image and filled with the own breath - this earthly trinity of man, woman and God would embark on the mission of being "fruitful, multiplying and subduing the earth". Genesis 1:28

Marriage was lovingly and purposefully designed by God and was never intended to be lived apart from Him. Man and wife, walking daily and deliberately in the presence and power of God, would experience life on earth in complete abundance and fulfillment, create and raise children who would marry with the same mission in mind - and all to the praise and glory of God.

This was God's plan. This was God's heart.

It still is.

Chapter Two

The Great Divorce

God's lavish plan for man and woman on earth had to be accompanied by one single caveat. One condition, upon which the fate of this perfect plan rested ...

His creation (man and woman) had to volunteer for duty. God loved them far too much to force them to accept and comply with His divine will for their lives, marriage and future. He had to allow them the opportunity to choose to love Him, to follow Him and to embrace His amazing plan for their lives. They were created with a personal and free will. God chose not to create them as robots, or droids who would automatically follow His every command. He designed them to make their own decisions and follow their own hearts.

God's love compelled Him to give His creation this ability to choose. It goes without saying, that He obviously desired for Adam and Eve to trust His heart and love for them and to choose wisely. As parents of three sons, my wife and I worked for years to teach them about their heavenly Father and to create a hunger in their hearts to want to know Him, seek His will and follow Him. All of our children, however, no matter how well we train them, must individually make the crucial choices that will shape their lives and futures.

I want my children to love me. I can't make them love me. I want to know they choose to love me and my heart leaps when I realize they do. My heart would break into a million pieces if I ever had reason to doubt it.

Love is a choice.

Love is voluntary. God made it that way. From the very first love story, Adam and Eve were given the freedom to choose to love God or not. We all know that love is more than a feeling and more than just words. Love is a verb. Love is action. Jesus reminds us that saying we love God is one thing, but truly loving Him is another -

> Jesus said, **"If you love me you will keep my commandments"** (John 14:15).

Adam and Eve were given the opportunity of a lifetime, "the" opportunity of all lifetimes. They could be the parents of a race of human beings who would know and walk with their Creator God and who would experience life on earth as it was intended. They had enjoyed the heaven-on-earth experience of knowing God personally and literally walking daily with Him. They had marveled at the unspoiled glory of His creation and had partnered with God in caring for it.

Can you even imagine a world without sin? A world without hate, shame, fear, hurt, pain, heartache, injustice, war, prejudice, disease, etc? That is almost unimaginable. Can you see the heart of a Father God who would create a world where that was possible, where that was the norm, where that was His desire for mankind?

That is the God of the Bible. That is the heart of the God who walked with Adam and Eve and desires to do the same with everyone who came from them - for all time.

Yet, that is also the God Who had to love mankind enough to give them the freedom to choose for themselves.

But ... there was evil in the Garden. This evil represented the "other" option. Genesis, chapter 3 describes for us the "serpent" who was *"more crafty than any of the other creatures the Lord God had made".* Ezekiel, chapter 28 and Revelation, chapter 12 provide an expanded explanation of who this "serpent" was and how he got there.

In the New Testament, Jesus calls the serpent "a liar and the father of lies" (John 8:44). Elsewhere he is referred to as "accuser" (Rev.12;10) and a "deceiver" (2 Cor. 11:3) who "blinds the minds of the unbelieving" (2 Cor. 4:4) and "enslaves" people (Titus 3:3). His primary mission, according to John 10 - is to "kill, steal and destroy" - especially those who call themselves "Christ-followers".

This serpent, Satan (Lucifer) was a beautiful and persuasive being. He was in the Garden with one intention - to thwart the plan of God. His sole purpose in life was (and still is) to steal God's glory and exalt himself instead. Whatever God is for - he is against. Whatever God loves - he hates. Whatever brings God glory - he is hell-bent on destroying.

Satan had also heard God's instructions to Adam in Genesis 2:15-17:

> Then the Lord God took the man and put him in the garden of Eden to tend and keep it. And the Lord God commanded the man, saying, "Of every tree of the garden you may freely eat; but of the tree of the knowledge of good and evil you shall not eat, for in the day that you eat of it you shall surely die."

He also knew that God had spoken directly to Adam and that Adam had relayed God's command to Eve. This would be his opening, his opportunity to do what he does best - lie, deceive, accuse, kill, steal, destroy.

So, rather than approaching Adam, who had had a much longer relationship with God and had heard God's command firsthand, Satan took the opportunity to engage sweet, innocent, relational Eve in conversation. Eve had never encountered this beautiful creature before (as far as we know) and was probably very intrigued that she could dialogue with another creature besides her husband. She had no idea of his diabolical intent and did not know there was such a thing as evil (having never eaten of that tree - Gen.2:16).

Satan's tactic was the same then as it is today - get them to doubt what God said, doubt His unconditional love and their ability to completely trust Him. His goal was to encourage them to think and act for themselves (independent of God's will).

Genesis 3:

> One day he (Satan) asked the woman, "Did God really say you must not eat the fruit from any of the trees in the garden?"

"Of course we may eat fruit from the trees in the garden," the woman replied. "It's only the fruit from the tree in the middle of the garden that we are not allowed to eat. God said, 'You must not eat it or even touch it; if you do, you will die.'"

"You won't die!" the serpent replied to the woman. "God knows that your eyes will be opened as soon as you eat it, and you will be like God, knowing both good and evil."

The woman was convinced. She saw that the tree was beautiful and its fruit looked delicious, and she wanted the wisdom it would give her. So she took some of the fruit and ate it. Then she gave some to her husband, who was with her, and he ate it, too.

"She was convinced". "She saw, she wanted, she took, she ate and she gave". We will talk much more about this later in the book, but I want you to notice the sequence. This sin of eternal significance began where all sin begins - in her mind, in her thoughts …

The Great Divorce?

As we have already seen, God created marriage. He brought Eve to Adam and the great marriage was performed. Life on planet earth was as it was designed to be … awesome.

Satan can't stand awesome. He hates "life as it should be". So he devised a plan to destroy what God intended for His glory and for man's delight.

Did all of this surprise God? Did it catch Him off guard? Not at all. But, God had to allow Adam and Eve to have a choice and He had to allow them to make their choice.

He made the rules (out of love) and they ignored them and chose to live life independently of what God wanted.

Have you ever given your child a command/rule to follow because you love them so much and you want only the best for them? Didn't it break your heart when they ignored it, or worse - deliberately disobeyed? The rule was there to protect them, not to inhibit them. It was there out of love, not for selfish control. As the parent, you know what is best for them, what will harm them and therefore out of love you set boundaries and make rules.

Imagine telling your young son not to run out into the busy street in front of your home to retrieve his new soccer ball. You explain how he could get hurt and because you love him deeply you have made such a rule. You tell Him to call you if the ball ever goes into the street and you will retrieve it for him.

Minutes later, from inside the house, you hear the sound of screeching brakes and a thud that will forever haunt you. You run to the street to find your son broken and bleeding. In your mind you are yelling "Why?" "Why didn't you listen to me?", "Why did you do that?" But your heart breaks as you hold your son and he says "I'm sorry daddy".

What if your son recovers but has to live the rest of his life confined to a wheelchair? A lifelong consequence for a choice made as a child. He was truly sorry, but the consequences can't be undone. Your heart broke when it happened, and it breaks every day since because he didn't believe you or trust your heart and your wisdom - and chose to do things his way instead of yours. If only ...

Out of great love, God made a rule. He also gave man the right to choose to follow that rule or not. He chose to disobey, to run out into the street, to do things his own way. He chose poorly.

Man's life became hard and not what God intended - God's heart broke.

Man didn't divorce his wife, but rather chose to divorce his first love - God.

He found another, someone he decided he loved more - himself.

And God's heart broke again.

Satan thought he had won; he had stolen God's bride (children) and His glory.

Thank goodness God had a master plan all along - a plan for reconciliation.

Chapter Three
The Reconciliation

The Bible again tells us that God's amazing love for us (mankind) compelled Him to do something else that broke His heart.

Genesis 3:22-24

> Then the Lord God said, "Look, the human beings have become like us, knowing both good and evil. What if they reach out, take fruit from the tree of life, and eat it? Then they will live forever!" So the Lord God banished them from the Garden of Eden, and he sent Adam out to cultivate the ground from which he had been made. After sending them out, the Lord God stationed mighty cherubim to the east of the Garden of Eden. And he placed a flaming sword that flashed back and forth to guard the way to the tree of life.

Because Adam and Eve had disobeyed God and chosen to go their independent way, God had no choice but to send them out of the gorgeous Garden they had always called home. More importantly (sadly), He was sending them away from Himself, from His presence. No longer would He walk with them and fellowship with them throughout the day as He had done all of their lives. As it would any parent, it had to break God's heart to have to impose the consequences He had promised if they were to disobey His one command.

The most devastating consequence of man's disobedience was being sent out into the world to live life apart from God's continual presence and involvement. The first couple chose independence and God was obliged to allow them to experience it.

Life, tainted by sin and selfishness, became much different for Adam and Eve. God was no longer physically there when they woke every morning, nor calling for them in the cool of the afternoon to discuss their day. They both felt nakedness, shame, fear, regret, anxiety and selfishness - for the first time in their lives. Disappointed in each other and disillusioned by their new life without God's direction, I'm sure they experienced their first marital problems. Their relationship, like everything else, became hard.

Life became hard.

Work became hard. Finding food, water, shelter, etc. was now up to them. God was not there to counsel them and guide them, to provide for them and protect them. No one else was to blame for their situation. Eve was deceived, but Adam was "with her" when that deception took place. He did not protect her, or lead her or encourage her to do what God had commanded. He went passive. Even though they were both at fault, God came to Adam for an explanation. Adam was created first. He was told directly by God what the rules were and also the consequences. The Bible also tells us that Adam was given the role as "head" of their home and their relationship (Eph. 5:23). Therefore, he was ultimately responsible for what happened.

From that time until the birth of Jesus, man's only option was to live life apart from the daily power and presence of God. God anointed some key people through the years and showed mankind His mighty power numerous times ... but the opportunity to walk daily in His presence was no longer an option. Man had made his choice.

Then, there was Christmas...

One day God declared "it is time". He began unveiling His master plan for the reconciliation of man to Himself. He initiated. He chose. He loved (verb) us so much that He did something.

Philippians 2:6-8

Though he (Jesus) was God, he did not think of equality with God as something to cling to. Instead, he gave up his divine privileges; he took the humble position of a slave and was born as a human being. When he appeared in human form, he humbled himself in obedience to God...

The Bible (Hebrews 1:3) says that Jesus is "the exact representation of God in human form". Jesus volunteered to become a human, but not just any human. He became the human who would be sacrificed in order to pay the penalty for the sin of Adam and Eve, and for all of us who would follow them. With our sin paid and our disobedience forgiven and forgotten - man would once again have the opportunity to re-enter Eden, as it were, with God. We would have the ability to experience and enjoy what we were created to enjoy - daily, continual fellowship with God.

"It is our deepest need, as human beings, to learn to live intimately with God. It is what we were made for". John Eldredge, Walking with God

Because Jesus paid the penalty for our disobedience, the gates to Eden are open wide once again. Gone is the physical Garden but the offer to experience personal, conversational intimacy with our Creator Father is as real today as it was in the beginning. God is present; God is speaking; God is leading; God is loving - just like in Eden. But.....

Just like Adam and Eve, we get to make a choice. Our choice is not whether to eat the forbidden fruit, however. Our choice is whether or not we will accept (receive/embrace) the sacrifice Jesus made by dying in our place on a cross and surrender our selfish desire to live life on our own terms, independent of God.

Will we trust our loving, Creator Father with our life, our marriage, our future or will we continue to listen to the serpent's voice telling us He cannot be trusted and that we know best how to run our own lives?

Once again, God allows us to decide - because He loves us.

What about marriage?

You see, those of us who accept/embrace/receive the sacrifice made by Jesus on our behalf - are called His people, His children, His church, His "bride"....

The Bible uses marriage as the primary metaphor to describe the relationship between Jesus and His church (His bride). His bride chose to leave Him and go her own way back in the Garden. But, out of His great love for her, He also made a choice. He chose to provide a way to win her back - to restore their relationship.

Even though His bride (we) wanted to have nothing to do with Him and showed no interest at all in reconciliation, Jesus initiated His plan and carried it out....

I Timothy 2:5-6

For there is one God, and one mediator
also between God and men, the man Christ Jesus,
who gave Himself as a ransom for all.

Romans 5:8

But God demonstrates His own love toward us, in that
while we were yet sinners, Christ died for us.

John 3:16

For God so loved the world (us) that He gave His only
begotten Son, that whosoever believes in Him should
not perish but have everlasting life.

Ephesians 2:1-9

And you were dead in your trespasses and sins, in
which you formerly walked according to the course of
this world, according to the prince of the power of
the air, of the spirit that is now working in the sons
of disobedience. Among them we too all formerly lived
in the lusts of our flesh, indulging the desires of the
flesh and of the mind, and were by nature children of
wrath, even as the rest. But God, being rich in mercy,
because of His great love with which He loved us,
even when we were dead in our transgressions, made
us alive together with Christ (by grace you have been
saved), and raised us up with Him, and seated us with
Him in the heavenly places in Christ Jesus, so that in
the ages to come He might show the surpassing riches
of His grace in kindness toward us in Christ Jesus.
For by grace you have been saved through faith; and
that not of yourselves, it is the gift of God; not as a
result of works, so that no one may boast.

Basically - we (the bride of Jesus) chose to leave His presence and live life on our own terms. We turned our back on Him and walked away. We didn't look back. We didn't want to reconcile...... but He did.

Jesus voluntarily suffered an excruciating death in order to pay the penalty for Adam and Eve's horrible choice. He loved us so much, He laid down His life so we wouldn't have to.

Romans 3:25

For God sent Christ Jesus to take the punishment for our sins and to end all God's wrath against us. He used Christ's blood and our faith as the means of saving us from his wrath.

We don't have to try to earn our way back to God, or live a life "good enough" for Him to love and accept us. Jesus did that for us, because He knows we could never do either. He reconciled us to God. He opened the gates of Eden for any of us who desire to once again experience the adventure of walking and talking with God.

He reconciled our relationship - our marriage. There is nothing any of us need to do in addition to what He has already done. But there remains yet another choice -

We must decide to come home. His sacrifice, His death, His reconciliation mean nothing if we don't make the choice to accept and embrace them.

There are no hard feelings. There is no penance we need to pay, no debt remains. His love never failed and we are completely, unconditionally forgiven. All we have to do is decide to turn around and come home.

Not everyone will make this choice, but for those who do - they will find a groom whose heart is filled with forgiveness, mercy and love. They will find the peace, joy and love they thought they could find on their own. They will find fulfillment, rest and the exhilarating communion of the Father they were created to enjoy - they will be home.

So - what does this all have to do with my marriage?

Great question. I'm glad you asked.

Remember Adam and Eve in the beginning of their relationship? They were overcome with joy to have each other as companions. They were completely naked, exposed and vulnerable with each other - and yet had no fear, no guilt, no shame. They were captivated with each other and captivated with God. Every day was an adventure.

They knew their Creator and He knew them. They walked together and talked together about the events of their days and about the future. What was ahead for them? What did God have in store?

They didn't approach each day with anxiety or fear or dread. Their marriage was awesome. Their relationship was perfect in every way. They couldn't wait to discover more of God's plan and experience the day He had made for them. They knew they were completely loved and they rested completely in God's heart for them and for their relationship.

Your life and your marriage were designed by the same, loving Father. He has an amazing plan for your life and marriage relationship that He longs to reveal to you and help you experience. Once again though - you get to decide whether you will trust Him or rely on your own wisdom, strength and abilities to come up with a plan of your own.

Until we come home, we will never experience marriage as it was intended to be experienced. We will have a void in our life and a hole in our heart that only being reconciled to our Father will fill. Our spouse will not fill it and was never intended to.

We will instinctively try to fill our void with work, hobbies, social media, fame, entertainment, vices and even ministry. We become frustrated with our spouse because he/she isn't meeting our need or making us happy. We may begin to believe that since they aren't filling the void in our heart (like we expected them to)...that they must be the problem.

Honestly, we are the problem. As long as we selfishly choose to live with our back to God, we will continue to live in need - of love, of fulfillment, of adventure, of joy and of significance ... but never fully find them. The hole in our soul remains. That is why second and third marriages have even higher and higher divorce rates.

Will we embrace Jesus' sacrifice and the opportunity to reconcile with God and walk daily with Him again? Will we embrace the opportunity to experience the presence and power of God in our marriage relationship?

All of us have been fully and completely reconciled to God. We have the opportunity to enjoy life - and marriage - as they were created and intended to be.

The choice is very clear, and actually pretty simple.

Just like in Eden - will we trust God or trust ourselves? Will we accept His offer of reconciliation or selfishly turn our backs and live life on our own terms?

Wait just a minute.

Are you saying the problems and issues in my marriage will simply vanish if I accept Christ's offer of redemption? Will being a Christ-follower magically make my life easier and my marriage fulfilling?

The short answer is … no. The long answer is … in the short term you may actually experience more difficulties.

What?

1 Corinthians 7:28

But those of you who marry will have
many troubles in this life.

The Bible speaks about all marriages having "many troubles/ trials" in this life. Anyone who has been married for longer than a day or two will agree - marriage is the most difficult relationship on the planet. You don't realize just how selfish you really are until you get married.

Because we all struggle with selfishness, we all will struggle in marriage. As you no doubt know by now, that was not God's original design for marriage. 1 Corinthians is simply stating the obvious - two selfish people, living in a fallen, broken, self-absorbed world - are going to struggle.

Without God's perspective; without God's Word we don't possess any knowledge that life and marriage can be anything but difficult. We all enter marriage feeling that "we are going to be different" and "our love is enough to see us through the hard times" - but it simply isn't true. Our strength, our hope, our love and even our best of intentions - just aren't good enough, or strong enough. It is little wonder that the percentage of marriages that divorce is still high. The percentage of marriages that are unfulfilling, unhappy, unsatisfying - is even higher.

Without God's perspective, we also have no hope that life and marriage could/should be anything but - hard as heck. We know of no better alternative so, when we finally have had enough, we leave, and try again. Or, for many, we settle for an average or "okay" marriage.

With God's perspective, we know that marriage was created by God and for God. It is not about us or our happiness. We embrace a higher calling for marriage than to meet our own selfish needs in life. Therefore, when things get hard (and they will) we have to choose against our very nature.

We have to choose to humble ourselves and follow God's plan, not our own. Instead of choosing to leave and try again, we choose to stay and fight. We choose to run to God and "*find grace to help in our time of need*" Hebrews 4:16.

What makes this so hard is that our flesh (our selfishness) is screaming for us to quit, to run, to take the path of least resistance - try to make ourselves happy.

That is why I say marriage, in the short term, can "feel" harder for the Christ-follower. Our flesh's gravitational field is pulling us away from each other. The enemy is trying to convince us that life will be easier, the grass is greener, and that we deserve better. The fight intensifies because you (as a follower) now know that God has a plan and it might be different than your plan.

In the longer term however, Christ-followers will find that God is a God of miracles, of power, or restoration and of second-chances. It is in Him that we finally find the power source that will sustain us through any trial or difficulty we face. Walking with Him, trusting Him will ultimately prove to us what the Bible preaches - He is good; He is faithful; He loves us; and He is all we need.

Life and marriage will not be less hectic or less challenging, but they will be richer, deeper and more fulfilling. You will be able to see God's hand in amazing ways. You will hear His voice and discover the abundant life He promised.

God has reconciled us to Himself. He longs for us to live life in His presence once again. Our choice to embrace the life we were created for - is our choice to make.

Not just once - but every day from now on.

> Then he called the crowd to him along with
> his disciples and said: "Whoever wants
> to be my disciple must deny themselves
> and take up their cross daily and follow me."
> Mark 8:34

Chapter Four
The 11th Commandment

We are all familiar with God's Ten Commandments. These "thou shall not's" have shaped our country's foundation, our society's conscience and our personal lives/relationships since God spoke them to Moses centuries ago. (see Exodus 20)

But there is an eleventh commandment that I want to draw your particular attention to. This commandment was given by Jesus and was given to us regarding our relationships. I believe it applies especially to that relationship closest to us - our marriage relationship.

Jesus was nearing the time of his death. He knew his time on earth was short and he took the time to do and say some very significant things. He gathered his disciples together for one last supper together. He reminded them for the last time that he was going to die and that they were to remember the significance of the bread and wine for generations to come.

He also demonstrated love (His definition - "agape" love) by disrobing and washing his disciples dirty, smelly feet. He wanted them to see for themselves what he had been trying so hard to tell them - love is a verb; it is something you do, something you choose; something you demonstrate.

Then he spoke something very significant to all who were present in the room. He called it *"a new commandment".* This, like the original ten, was not merely a godly suggestion. His use of the terms "new" and "commandment" were significant. This message was as important as the one spoken by God to Moses, but it was different, it was new - so listen closely.

John 13:34
A new commandment I give to you,
that you love one another, even as I have
loved you, that you also love one another.

Since this is a book about marriage - I want to point out three very significant things in what Jesus said:

1. This is a commandment - and commandments are significant. This is required behavior, expected behavior, consequential behavior - expected of us. If you knew you had hours to live and brought together your family and closest friends one last time - don't you think you would give significant thought and weight to the things you would want to tell them? As we have already seen, marriage was created by God and is incredibly important to Him. We are to pay significant heed to what He says about it.

2. We are to love one another. Yeah, yeah we are supposed to love one another, that's not really new news is it? What we must understand is the Greek word Jesus uses for "love" in this command is the word "agape". This is

the highest form of love, God's kind of love. This is not emotional, feelings-based "eros" love, or brotherly/friendship "phileo" kind of love, but the kind of love that is a choice of the lover and has nothing to do with the one being loved; a choice-based love; "agapeo" or agape kind of love is the kind of love God loves us with ... and aren't we glad.

3. We are to love one another "as I have loved you". As mentioned in #2 above, this kind of love is not based on performance or feelings, but on an act of the will, a choice to love. It has nothing to do with someone's performance, response, or their ability to love in return. Remember how Jesus loved us. He initiated love when we didn't love him; He gave his own life in order to restore our fellowship and right standing before God; He humbled himself, He served, He gave, He sacrificed - He died. And ... not because we deserved it or loved him in return. He just did.

And now He tells us that this is the way we are to love each other. Have you heard the phrase "fell out of love", or heard someone say they were getting a divorce because "they grew apart" and just "didn't love each other anymore"? Which of the three types of love do you suppose those excuses fall under?

God's love (agapeo) is not a feeling; it is not contingent on anything - not your spouse's response or performance or whether you think he/she deserves it. It's not based on how you feel about your spouse.

Did we deserve Jesus' love? Do we now? Is His love for us based on our performance or good works - or how much we love Him in return? Thank goodness it's not.

The truth is - we so appreciate the way God loves us, but we don't really want to love our spouse by the same standard. We don't want to obey this "new commandment". We are very good at monitoring our spouse's behavior (what they do and don't do, say and don't say) and demanding performance from them (but not necessarily from ourselves). *"I will set aside time with her as soon as she meets my need for sexual fulfillment". "I will be more engaged in meeting his needs when he starts meeting mine". "I will respect him when he becomes more respectable" ... "If he/she will, I will".*

Some of us actually like pouting and/or manipulating. We like holding out on our spouse until they "shape up" or "see things our way". Like three-year-olds we fold our arms and stomp our feet and stick out our bottom lip - until we get our way. If that doesn't work, we trying nagging, yelling, retreating, the quiet treatment, cutting off sex, etc. Sound familiar?

Basically, we are just selfish.

It is the way we are all born. We wake up every morning and our default view of life is switched to "me". Everyone from our spouse, to our children, the morning traffic, the weather, the drive thru at Starbucks and our co-workers should know that my needs, desires, goals and expectations should be met first, and at all cost. Ouch - sometimes the truth hurts.

You were probably different than me - but if I'm honest, I would have to admit that hiding somewhere deep in my love-smitten heart when I got married at age twenty two was the totally selfish expectation that my wife would make "me" happy and meet "my" needs.

For a day or two this worked out pretty well for me. Then I had to face the reality that she had needs and expectations of her very own. As a Christian I turned to the Bible for answers. I was sure to find some logical, reasonable compromise that could be reached. After all, God is a God of fairness, right?

While studying the topic of "love" (since that is what I got married for anyway), it didn't take long to encounter the love that compelled Jesus to voluntarily sacrifice his life in order to rescue us from eternal darkness and provide us the opportunity to enjoy an abundant, fulfilling life possible both now and for eternity.

Jesus not only spoke of God's love, "agape" love - he showed me what it looked like. He loved me unconditionally, totally, without any prerequisites or conditions on my part. He showed me what love is and then told me to love my bride the very same way.

As much as I loved my new wife naturally, I had no clue how to love her supernaturally. How was I supposed to love her the same way Jesus loves me? Seriously, all he asks is for me to:

give myself up for her; nourish and cherish her; do not be harsh with her; be considerate of her; treat her with respect; handle her with utmost care; respect her as God's daughter, and His personal provision for me. Be the head, the leader, the initiator in our relationship; Make her my top priority every day; Live in harmony with her; be sympathetic, be compassionate, be humble; not repay evil for evil or insult for insult; desire peace and pursue it; be devoted to her; honor her above myself; be patient; not envy; not be prideful; not be rude; not be selfish; not be easily angered; not keep score; delight in the truth; not let any unwholesome word come out of my mouth; be kind and compassionate; forgive her "as Christ has forgiven me"; consider her better than myself; look out for her interests; have the same attitude as Jesus; be gentle; patient; bear with her; not love with words only but also with action and with truth; voluntarily lay my life down ... die to myself.

What a shock wave to the very core of my selfish soul.

What about me? What about my needs and my desires?

And yeah, what about her? What is she supposed to do … for me?

His answer? " It's not about you. You are responsible to obey me and do what I command you to do as a husband - irregardless of her response. You do what you are supposed to do and I will take care of her".

How am I supposed to pull this off? Surely He is aware of all that is going on in my life right now. Surely He sees that I need to catch a break. With all that I am juggling right now, does He really expect me to love my spouse like He loves His bride? It's not that I don't want to, I just really can't spare the time. I am so busy - I'm sure that can wait until things ease up a bit, right?

Yes, Jesus does know who you are and what you're dealing with right this very minute. He loves you, and wants only the best for you - but, His commandments are still valid, and His Word is still our blueprint for successful relationships.

In God's blueprint, there are no "ifs", or "whens" or "buts". We are commanded to follow His example and love "just like" He loves us. Our actions can never be contingent on our spouse's actions, response or performance. If they are, then we are not loving with "agape" love. Worse still - we are choosing to disobey God's 11th commandment - and our marriage will suffer because of it.

As with Adam and Eve, the choice is ours. The blessings or consequences are ours too.

Will we choose to obey Him or turn our back and simply hope He doesn't see?

Chapter Five

The Impossible Assignment

I remember an assignment in high school that I thought was impossible. The teacher assigned us an oral book report on the book of our own choice. She gave us several weeks to read it and prepare, but being the athletically and socially active jock that I was, I didn't make this report a top priority....until I remembered the assignment the weekend before it was due... on Monday. Yes, Monday morning I was scheduled to stand in front of my peers and give an oral report on the book I had read.

How could my teacher give me such an impossible task? This was SO unfair.

My quick thinking and ability to recall a combination of war movies I had seen on television helped me piece together a plausible enough storyline to a fictitious book (and author). I should probably confess this sin to my former English teacher, but I'm sure she is in heaven by now.

Yes, I made up a book. I made up an author. I basically made up a story too. But, it was good enough for a "B" grade ... and I was relieved.

You see, the assignment wasn't impossible. Challenging maybe but not impossible. What made it seem impossible was my choice to indulge myself instead of reading a "real" book and working on the report during the assigned timeframe. Since I chose to be a slacker, the assignment grew to impossible proportions and made my life much more difficult.

The same can be said for our marriage. Not impossible if taken a day at a time and if you work at it along the way. After the honeymoon glow wears off (and it does wear off) the reality of trying to meet another person's needs for a lifetime can truly seem impossible.

Marriage is God's ultimate workshop.

We never know how truly selfish we are until we get married. God uses our spouse as His primary hand tool to assist Him in slowly shaping us into His likeness.

As I hope you have already seen, God didn't create marriage to be frustrating, exhausting, disheartening, unfulfilling and hard. He created it to be His primary instrument for bringing Him glory and advancing His kingdom on earth. But, as you have also seen, that all changed with one bite of an apple.

Yet, to God marriage should be our most sacred and satisfying relationship on this planet. It is at the same time both exhilarating and exhausting; full of mountain tops and lonely valleys; wondrous joys and deep disappointments. Enjoying a truly satisfying relationship with another selfish person, 24/7, three hundred sixty five days a year - for a lifetime - is a miracle of Red Sea proportions.

And remember, the goal is not to simply stick it out, tie a rope around each other and drag each other to the finish line. The goal is joy. The goal is experiencing God in ways neither could comprehend alone. The mission is not just to finish the race but to run well, to bring Him great glory and ourselves deep fulfillment in the process.

The achievement of those goals comes from living every day in such a way as to fulfill His new commandment - to love "as He loves".

His Word offers us further, more specific instructions as to what this kind of love actually looks like. There are more commandments and many instructions that may seem like an impossible mission at first glance, but we will see later that once again - God has a master plan that is awesome and achievable.

Here are some additional commands given specifically to <u>husbands</u>:

1 Corinthians 7:2-5

In the same way, the husband's body does not belong to him alone but also to his wife. Do not deprive each other...

Ephesians 5:25-33

Husbands love your wives, just as Christ loved the church and gave himself up for her.... However, each one of you also must love his wife as he loves himself...

Colossians 3:19

Husbands, love your wives and do not be harsh with them.

1 Peter 3:7-12

Husbands, in the same way be considerate as you live with your wives, treat them with respect as the weaker partner and as heirs with you of the grace of life, so that nothing will hinder your prayers.

So Guys - let's stop for a minute and ask the obvious questions based on the previously-mentioned verses:

- *Are you keeping your body from your wife? My bet is, you're making it very available for sex, but have you ever thought that this verse could also mean other things too? What about your arms/legs - are you quick to help out around the house, or with the kids - even if you prefer to watch the game, or go hit golf balls? Are you giving your wife your eyes, ears and mouth? Are you engaging with her in meaningful conversation, listening to her heart and offering words of encouragement and support? Do you regularly pray with her.*

- *Are you loving (verb) your wife "as" Christ loves his bride by giving yourself up for her? Are you deliberate about putting her needs above your own? Do you sacrifice your wants and desires for her on a regular basis, and without whining or keeping score?*

- *Do you love your wife with your words? Ask her for her definition of "harsh". Then ask God to help you never be that way with her, and ask her to tell you if you ever are? If so - quickly say you're sorry and ask her to forgive you.*

- *Do you treat her with the upmost respect? She is God's daughter and His personal gift to you. Do you treat her accordingly? If not - your prayers will be "hindered" (thwarted, ineffective), and you really don't want that.*

You see how this works? We (husbands) have been given instructions by God regarding how He wants/expects us to treat His daughter. We will be accountable to Him for how well we do this ... or not.

This requires thought. This requires planning and action. This requires a daily, deliberate choosing on our part - to live our lives this way. Or you know as well as I do, it won't happen. Our natural tendency is to sit back and assume all will work out fine on its own. We would prefer not to have to work at it - and somehow enjoy a fabulous marriage.

Now, the wives' turn. Here are some additional commands given specifically to <u>wives</u>:

1 Corinthians 7:2-5

The wife's body does not belong to her alone but also to her husband. Do not deprive each other...

Ephesians 5:22-24

Wives, submit to your husbands as unto the Lord...

Ephesians 5:33

However, each one of you also must love his wife as he loves himself, and the wife must respect her husband.

1 Peter 3:1-6

Wives, in the same way be submissive to your husbands so that if any of them do not believe the word...

So Ladies - let's stop for a minute and ask the obvious questions based on the previously-mentioned verses:

- *Are you keeping your body from your husband? Is sexual intimacy and time connecting physically a major priority in your life, or an obligatory afterthought because "he needs it"? Do you ever use sex with your husband, or the lack of it, as a tool to get him to perform for you? Are your actively engaging him in respectful, encouraging conversation? Are you showing him non-sexual, physical touch (affection) and letting him know he is still your #1 man?*

- *Are you voluntarily submitting to him as the "head" of the home, or do you step in and run things when he isn't leading the way you would prefer? Have you read/studied what the Bible means by "submission" or have you passed that notion off as not being valid in our current culture?*

- *Do you regularly show respect for your husband by your words and actions? Are you waiting for him to become more "respectable" before you obey what God says? Should he wait to love you until you become more lovable?*

- *God will use your submissive, encouraging attitude to draw your husband closer to Him. He will use your example more than your words. Look for your fulfillment in Christ, not your husband.*

- *Are you trying to be the Holy Spirit to your husband or are you content to trust God with His growth?*

Here is some of God's teaching on relationships that are even more pertinent in the context of our marriage relationship. Stop after reading each verse and ask God if it describes the way you love (verb) your spouse …

Romans 12:10

Be devoted to one another in brotherly love.
Honor one another above yourselves.

1 Corinthians 7:33

But a married man is concerned about the affairs
of this world – how he can please his wife.

1 Corinthians 11:24

Let no one seek his own good, but that
of his neighbor (spouse).

Ephesians 4:29, 32

Let no unwholesome talk come out of your mouth but only
what is helpful for building others up … Be kind and
compassionate to one anther, forgiving one another,
just as Christ forgave you.

Philippians 2:3-5

Do nothing out of selfish ambition or vain conceit, but in humility consider others better than yourselves. Do not only look out for your own interests but also to the interests of others. Your attitude should be the same as that of Christ Jesus.

Colossians 3:12-13

As God's chosen people, clothe yourselves with compassion, kindness, humility, gentleness and patience. Bear with one another ... forgive as the Lord forgave you.

1 Peter 3:8-12

Finally, all of you, live in harmony with one another; be sympathetic, love as brothers, be compassionate and humble. Do not repay evil for evil or insult for insult, but with blessing....turn from evil and do good, seek peace and pursue it.

1 John 3:18

Dear children, let us not love with words or tongue, but with actions and in truth.

Are you regularly obeying God's eleventh commandment?

When you open your eyes every morning, are your first thoughts of asking God to help you please your spouse today? Do you always honor your spouse's desires/needs above your own? Are you naturally kind, compassionate, humble, patient, forgiving, gentle, etc?

Would your spouse say that you regularly show him/her love (agape) by your actions?

Wow! How does someone actually pull that off? That's impossible.

Does God really expect us to <u>live</u> like that, to <u>act</u> like that - to <u>be</u> like that?

The short answer is - yes.

But before you throw your hands up and give up - or worse yet, never even try ...

... read on.

Chapter Six
The Divine Calling

As we have already seen in Chapter 4, there is a divine calling on every husband and every wife who claim to be children, disciples, followers of Jesus:

John 13:34

A new commandment I give to you, that you
love one another; as I have loved you,
that you also love one another.

Each of us is called, yes - commanded, to love our spouse. It seems that many couples today simply stop there ... **sure, I love my wife/husband**. Many divorced couples will say they still "love" their ex, but just can't live together. We continue to define "love" by our own standards or by what the world says is "normal" or "acceptable".

As a Christian spouse, however, we do not have that luxury. God holds us to a much higher standard - His standard. There is no argument, no compromise, no acceptable excuse. One day He will ask each us how we did. We will stand before Him and give an account of how well we "loved" our spouse - based on His standard.

So if we are to love "as Jesus loved us" - what does that look like? Wouldn't it make sense to look at Jesus' life to see how he did it?

Philippians 2: 6-8

who, though he was in the form of God, did not regard equality with God as something to be exploited, but emptied himself, taking the form of a slave, being born in human likeness. And being found in human form, he humbled himself and became obedient to the point of death even death on a cross.

Jesus' love compelled him to do something; initiate; rescue his bride (church) from a sentence of death/hell. This verse tells us that he:

1. **Emptied himself** - he left the glory of heaven and his deity behind - he became a dependent and vulnerable human being.

2. **Humbled himself** - he became dependent on his parents and especially on God - he messed his diaper, learned to walk, he went to school, he learned a trade - he worked, he went to church and he helped provide for his family. He served the very people who would one day betray him, mock, torture and kill him.

3. **Became obedient** - he had to wait for God's timing before beginning his ministry - he learned to walk with God, pray, listen and obey God's voice. He understood that he *"could do nothing on his own"* (see John 5) but was desperate to hear from God, every day. Hebrews 5:8 tells us that Jesus *"learned obedience through the things he suffered".*

Matthew 20:26-28

it will not be so among you; but whoever wishes to be great among you must be your servant, and whoever wishes to be first among you must be your slave; just as the Son of Man came not to be served but to serve, and to give his life a ransom for many.

Jesus' love compelled him to serve instead of expecting to be served. He laid down his life in order to ransom/save/rescue our lives from a death sentence. He provided for and protected his bride (us) even when we didn't desire it, expect it or deserve it.

John 10:18

No one can take my life from me.
I sacrifice it voluntarily.

Jesus' love compelled him to give his life away - literally. The Creator of life voluntarily gave his life away because of love. He made the choice. He showed us real love, "agape" love; love not based on feelings but on choice. I'm sure his human emotions and feelings weren't really excited about the impending pain, anguish and humiliation of a suffocating death on a cross - yet, knowing all of that, he still chose that route.

The love that Jesus loved us with (and still loves us with) is a love worth dying for. He loved His bride so much that He gave His life for her (us). That is the love we are called to. That is agape love - God's love.

Before you believe the lie that just flashed through your mind - that *you can't possibly love that way, you can't love like God* - let me remind you that God will never call us, or command us, to do something that He will not empower us to do.

Philippians 2:13

for it is God who is at work in you, both to will and to
do of His good pleasure.

John 17:26

and I have made Your name known to them, and will make
it known, so that the love with which You loved Me may be
in them, and I in them.

Acts 1:8

but you will receive power when the Holy Spirit
has come upon you; and you shall be My witnesses
both in Jerusalem, and in all Judea and Samaria,
and even to the remotest part of the earth.

1. God now lives in you through His Holy Spirit

2. He will work in you to both will and do the things He asks
   you to do

3. The will to obey His commands and the power to obey them
   - come from the same Holy Spirit.

So, yes - in our own strength, we are helpless to ever love our
spouse with God's agape love. In our own strength we cannot
consistently choose against our self-centeredness and maintain
relationships based on God's standards.

But, **if** we are willing to do what Jesus asks us to do - deny
ourselves, take up our cross every day (die) and follow Him -
we have a 100% chance of enjoying marriage as it was created
and intended to be enjoyed. That is why the famous and often-
quoted marriage passage in Ephesians 5:21-33 actually begins
in verse 15:

Be very careful, then, how you live—not as unwise
but as wise, making the most of every opportunity,
because the days are evil. Therefore do not be foolish,
but understand what the Lord's will is. Do not get
drunk on wine, which leads to debauchery. Instead,
be filled with the Spirit, speaking to one another
with psalms, hymns, and songs from the Spirit.
Sing and make music from your heart to the Lord,
always giving thanks to God the Father for everything,
in the name of our Lord Jesus Christ.

Unless husbands and wives are filled with God's Spirit, they will never be able to do what is commanded in the following verses. This is not a one-time event, but a daily choice we make to humble ourselves and submit to His Lordship in our lives and in our marriage.

But a husband and wife who are willing to lay down their individual rights and "deserve-its" (deny themselves), die to their personal agendas (take up their cross) and follow Jesus (not the world, culture, or their own feelings or inclinations) - will enjoy an extraordinary marriage that is marked by what the Bible calls the "fruit of the Spirit" in Galatians 5:

love, joy , peace, patience, kindness, goodness,
faithfulness, gentleness and self control.

Isn't that the kind of fruit every marriage actually wants to enjoy?

When my wife and I married forty years ago I thought that beautiful spiritual fruit would magically appear in my life by "being a nice guy; a church-going guy; a guy who asked Christ into his life at age 17". I would read my Bible occasionally, attend church religiously, and had sincere intentions to live a fruitful life. The sad truth is that I continued to fall woefully short ... again and again.

I would hear a powerful sermon on how I should treat my wife or take copious notes at a marriage conference and once again pledge to "do" those things, and "be" that kind of man for her. Then, "BAM"- flat on my face only days later.

I am sad to admit that it took me way too long to finally understand that it was not about my sincerity or my trying harder. It was about letting go, dying to myself and surrendering to God's Spirit in my life. It was about allowing Him to do what He does best - love people - and love my wife through me. I had to learn how to have a marriage worth dying for.

Jesus' love never leaves; never lets go. Think about all the times you have disappointed Christ, let Him down, sinned against Him and broken His heart. He never leaves us there. His love:

> is patient, is kind. It does not envy, it does not boast, it is not proud. It does not dishonor others, it is not self-seeking, it is not easily angered, it keeps no record of wrongs. It does not delight in evil but rejoices with the truth. It always protects, always trusts, always hopes, always perseveres.
> His love never fails.

1 Corinthians 13:4-8

I am certain that our behavior and our choices often break the Lord's heart. I am continuously reminded and thankful that Christ chose to leave heaven and suffer an excruciating death for me when I was "dead" spiritually. I didn't care about God. I wasn't looking for Him. I didn't love Him or earn His love in any way. He simply chose to love me, rescue me, and offer me an eternity of joy in His presence.

Because of His sacrificial death, the Bible says that I have been adopted into His family, forever, and nothing and no one will ever change that.

Ephesians 1:4-5

Even before he made the world, God loved us and chose us in Christ to be holy and without fault in his eyes. God decided in advance to adopt us into his own family by bringing us to himself through Jesus Christ. This is what he wanted to do, and it gave him great pleasure.

It also says that nothing and no one can separate us from His amazing love.

Romans 8:38-39

For I am convinced that neither death nor life, neither angels nor demons, neither the present nor the future, nor any powers, neither height nor depth, nor anything else in all creation, will be able to separate us from the love of God that is in Christ Jesus our Lord.

Jesus' love for us compelled Him to choose us, adopt us, and never be separated from us - all before we even knew about Him or accepted His love for ourselves. As a believer, we are His children and will always be. There is nothing we can do to change that. He is always with us, always listening, always caring, always willing to help.

Lastly, Jesus' love prays.

Romans 8:26-27, 31-32

In the same way the Spirit also helps our weakness; for we do not know how to pray as we should, but the Spirit Himself intercedes for us with groanings too deep for words; and He who searches the hearts knows what the mind of the Spirit is, because He intercedes for the saints according to the will of God.

What then shall we say to these things? If God is for us, who is against us? He who did not spare His own Son, but delivered Him over for us all, how will He not also with

Him freely give us all things? Who will bring a charge
against God's elect? God is the one who justifies; who is
the one who condemns? Christ Jesus is He who died, yes,
rather who was raised, who is at the right hand of God,
who also <u>intercedes for us.</u>

Jesus sits at the right hand of God - and prays for us. You and me. He keeps on loving us by praying for us every day. Can you fathom the Son of God sitting beside the Father God, praying for your marriage - right now as you read this? Wow.

And to top it off, the Holy Spirit of God (who is living inside each of us as believers) also "intercedes for us with groanings too deep for words" and prays to the Father on our behalf "according to the will of God".

We don't pray like that! We don't pray continually. Heck, many of us don't pray much at all. We sure don't pray with groanings too deep for words. We don't cry out to the Father day after day and always according to His will and His Word. Doesn't that blow your mind? It does mine.

THE DIVINE CALLING on each of our lives as married couples - is to love each other like that. Like Jesus loved us. Like Jesus still loves us.

Each of us is called by God to "empty ourself", "humble ourself" and "obey God" - even unto our death. Unlike Jesus, this will most likely not be our physical death, but will most definitely be our emotional death. As I have mentioned, we are called to make the daily choice to die to our own agendas, independence and rights. This is the "cross" we agreed to take up when we said "I do" to Christ and when we vowed to love, honor and serve our spouse "till death do us part".

So, the question is - are we doing this?

Is your marriage worth dying for? According to God it is. So, if you find yourself at a time in your relationship that is less than satisfying or fulfilling, it's time to look vertically not horizontally.

If you are not seeing the fruit you desire, it's time to examine whether or not you are truly walking in the Spirit.

Remember - it's not your spouse's fault (Adam tried the blame game before), and God will always remind you that it is your responsibility to walk in the Spirit and obey what He has commanded you.

Most of the marital "issues" my wife and I have encountered over the years in counseling/mentoring other couples have their root cause here.

Most Christian couples simply don't deliberately, consistently walk with God. A new book, DVD series or small group study will never produce the fruit we all so desperately seek in our marriage. It's actually very simple - will we choose to spend time with, listen to, obey and walk with God every day or not? If we selfishly choose "not", then we only have ourselves to blame for a mediocre or unfulfilling marriage.

You know another wonderful thing I love about our God? Contrary to what our enemy would have us believe, He doesn't saddle us with impossible rules and then sit back and wait for us to screw up, so He can zap us.

Actually, it is just the opposite ...

Chapter Seven
The Inexhaustible Resource

Remember the oral book report I made up in Chapter 5? I had all the resources I needed to create and deliver that report. The truth is - I just didn't avail myself of them. The same is true about our marriage. We have everything we need to make our marriage everything we want it to be - IF we will take advantage of them.

There is an insidious lie that has been prevalent in Christian circles for years that what we need is more information, more equipping. More books, dvds, small group studies and sermons on marriage will certainly provide the answers we need to enjoy marriage as God intended, and stem the rising tide of divorce.

As wonderful and necessary as these resources are, they are not the answer for long-term, sustainable joy and fulfillment in marriage. Jesus never asked us to learn more principles and attempt to apply them - *He asked us to follow a person* - Him. The Pharisees knew a lot of truth. They memorized and studied their Bible. But, Jesus sternly rebuked them for not knowing the real Truth - Him. (John 5:39-40).

He created each of us, He created marriage - surely He will supply everything we need to enjoy it. If we follow God's blueprint we have a 100% chance of enjoying an extraordinary marriage.

The sad reality is this - we don't follow well.

My good friend, Robbie Linn, always says, *"the hardest thing about being a Christ-follower ... is following Christ".*

But that is all Jesus ever asked us to do. Check this out -

Mark 1:16-18

Jesus was walking by the Sea of Galilee. He saw Simon and his brother Andrew putting a net into the sea. They were fishermen. Jesus said to them, "Follow Me. I will make you fish for men!" At once they left their nets and followed Him.

Mark 8:34-35

Jesus called the people and His followers to Him. He said to them, "If anyone wants to be My follower, he must give up himself and his own desires. He must take up his cross and follow Me. If anyone wants to keep his own life safe, he will lose it. If anyone gives up his life because of Me and because of the Good News, he will save it.

The amazing truth revealed in the Mark 1 passage is this: Our "job" is to follow Jesus. His "job" is to "make us". He never told anyone they had to clean up their act, or learn more truth or never sin again in order to be his follower. He simply asked them to follow. He said if we would do that, He would do the rest. He would "make us" what He desires us to be. He will not force that upon us though. Like we have already seen with Adam and Eve, we are given free will, we are given a choice - follow or not.

Following - is used in the Bible to describe what a believer, a disciple, a Christian does. "Christ-follower" is who they are.

John 10:27

My sheep hear My voice and I know them. They follow Me.

John 10:26

If anyone wants to serve Me, he must follow Me. So where I am, the one who wants to serve Me will be there also.

Implicit in Jesus' words is the relationship of leader-follower; rabbi-disciple; skilled craftsman-apprentice, shepherd-sheep. These types of relationships were commonplace in those times and a normal and necessary part of their culture. How else was a young man to learn the ways of life, or of work and business?

Jesus specifically said, if someone claims to be my disciple - they WILL follow me. They will walk with me, stay close to me, listen and pay attention to what I say and strive to live as I live.

Also implied in Jesus' words was the cultural reality that following costs something. A true disciple paid a price to follow. Like the disciples of Jesus, they left their former life behind when they chose to follow. They walked away from family, jobs and friends to follow their leader/teacher. They denied and/or delayed their own plans, hopes and dreams. They "died" to their agenda for their life. This was the "cross" Jesus spoke of when he said:

Matthew 10:38

He who does not take his cross and follow Me is not good enough for Me.

Luke 9:23

Then Jesus said to them all, "If anyone wants to follow Me, he must give up himself and his own desires. He must take up his cross everyday and follow Me.

Luke 14:27

If he does not carry his cross and follow Me, he cannot be My follower.

It was with this in mind that Jesus called his disciples (followers) and pledged to them that if they would truly follow - He would make them into the men He intended them to become. He would do his part if they would do theirs - follow.

But, as the disciples quickly learned (and Jesus already knew) - following is hard.

Recently on a men's retreat we were asked to partner with another man for a practical application of this truth. One man was blindfolded and asked to lightly hold on to their partner's shirt as they both navigated some rough outdoor terrain. Creeks, fallen limbs, tree stumps and rocks were only a few of the dangers each pair had to navigate in order to make it to a finish line.

I remember as the blindfolded man how dependent I was on my partner to lead me, speak to me about the terrain ahead and when/where to step in order to avoid danger. I could see nothing and was completely dependent on my partner. I had to hold on to him, listen to his voice and do what he said if I was going to safely finish.

Following was hard. It was work. But what it required of me was primarily three things: trust my leader, listen to him and do what he said.

What continues to overwhelm me regarding my own life and my marriage - is that Jesus makes me the very same offer he made the disciples. He makes it to you as well:

"Follow me, and I will make you" ...

- the man of God I have always wanted to be (and He wants me to be)

- the husband I desire to be and my wife deserves

- the father my boys need to model for them the life of a fully devoted follower of Jesus

Jesus is everything I need and He has all the resources, power, wisdom, time and desire to "make me" into the man He created me to become.

Philippians 4:19

And my God will meet all your needs according to the riches of his glory in Christ Jesus.

Philippians 4:13

I can do all things through Christ who strengthens me.

Matthew 6:33

Seek first the kingdom of God and His righteousness, and all these things will be added unto you

1 Timothy 6:17

Instruct those who are rich in this present world not to be conceited or to fix their hope on the uncertainty of riches, but on God, who richly supplies us with all things to enjoy.

As a believer, a Christ-follower, a disciple, we have access to an incomprehensible, inexhaustible resource. In the four verses we just read we are promised -

- He **will provide all** (not some) of my needs.

- **I can do all things** through Him.

- **All these things** will be added unto me if I put Him first in my life.

- He richly (not barely) **supplies me with all things** to enjoy.

We have a mentor, a teacher, a shepherd unlike any who has ever lived or ever will live. Everything we need in order to enjoy an abundantly fruitful and fulfilling life and an extraordinary marriage are found in one Person.

He never asked us to try harder or learn more or straighten our lives out before He would be willing to help us. All He asks of us is the same thing he has asked people for centuries ...

Follow me.

Where I got way off track was not understanding what those two words really meant. As a new believer at age 17, I thought following Jesus meant 1) going to church, 2) reading my Bible occasionally, and 3) being a "good" guy - i.e.: giving up drinking, lusting, lying, cursing, etc.

While I was close, it took me years to understand that following Christ wasn't about being religious (do's and don'ts), but about a relationship. It's not about church attendance, tithing, giving up vices or even "having a quiet time" ... but following a person.

So, what does that look like?

Volumes have been written on this subject, so I will focus my thoughts to three essential actions that I believe characterize the life of a true follower:

1. They are captivated by the extravagant love of God.

2. They have come to realize that they can accomplish nothing without Him.

3. They are passionate about staying close to Him, hearing His voice and doing what He tells them to do.

First, I am convinced that until you truly embrace (not just mentally acknowledge) the deep, unconditional love of God - for YOU - it will always be difficult for you to embrace the love of a spouse and be able to unselfishly love him/her well. ***You can't give what you don't have***, the old saying goes.

I have loved my wife since before high school, but I did not truly know what loving her with God's kind of love (agape) was until years into our marriage. After we began having children I began to realize what unconditional love looked like in real life. I loved my sons whether they spit up on my shoulder, filled their diaper with nuclear fallout, misbehaved or willingly disobeyed. I loved them - period. I still do. Nothing will ever change that - ever.

God finally broke through my hard head years later when He convinced me that He loved me the very same way. Not because I deserved it, or had been a "good guy" or for any reason at all. He loved me - period. He still loves me. He even likes me. Every day He desires my company. He actually thinks about me -

Psalm 139: 17-18

How precious also are Your thoughts about me, O God!
How vast is the sum of them!

If I should count them, they would outnumber the sand.
When I awake, I am still with You.

Can you imagine? Do you realize that God actually thinks about you that much? I don't know about you, but I was blinded to that truth for far too many years. Just like God hung out with Adam every day, He desires to do the very same thing with me and you.

He loves us and there is nothing we can do to make Him love us any more, or any less, than He already does. Don't let the enemy rob you of that liberating truth!

His love for you is not contingent on your past behavior or your future performance. Take a minute and meditate on that. Don't believe the lies that tell you otherwise or that your situation is different. Moses committed murder; David too, and was an adulterer; Peter was impulsive and denied Christ, and Paul was a violent persecutor of the church. And yet, God loved them and used them to change history.

Embracing the Father's unconditional love will liberate your soul. Knowing you no longer have to perform, or tap dance for God's approval (or to avoid His punishment) will send a rush of fresh air into your sails like nothing else. You are loved, accepted, wanted, thought of, enjoyed and sought after....by a Father who has loved you, and will love you, like no one on earth ever has or ever will.

Walking in this truth will allow you to let go of the guilt and shame from your past and begin to walk in freedom. Freedom to live in the light of His presence; to never be ashamed again; and to walk with your head held high, a beloved son/daughter of the King of heaven.

Walking in this truth will also allow you to stop focusing on yourself and your needs and begin to focus on your spouse's. Now you can begin to learn to put his/her needs ahead of your own and to love like Christ loves you - unconditionally - in spite of your feelings - and irregardless of his/her response or performance. You will become a different husband, a different wife - because you are finally enjoying a life lived in the presence and power of God. And, as the Bible promises:

Psalm 16:11

You will make known to me the path of life;

In Your presence is fullness of joy;

In Your right hand there are pleasures forever.

The **second** great awakening every Christ-follower must have, is the same one acknowledged by Jesus when He walked the earth as a human:

John 5:19

Therefore Jesus answered and was saying to them, "Truly, truly, I say to you, the Son can do nothing of Himself, unless it is something He sees the Father doing; for whatever the Father does, these things the Son also does in like manner.

Jesus, in human form, realized that he could do nothing on his own. He had no super powers or extraordinary enablement from God. He was like us - human, vulnerable.

Hebrews 4:15

For we do not have a high priest who cannot sympathize with our weaknesses, but One who has been tempted in all things as we are, yet without sin.

Jesus realized early in his life and early in his ministry that he did not have the wisdom, strength or power to do what he was sent to do. He needed help. He needed his Father. *He was desperate for God*; desperate for His wisdom; desperate for His power; desperate for His direction.

Doesn't that sound familiar? Don't you find yourself in situations nearly every day where you need the same things? I sure do. Sadly, my default setting is to call on my own wisdom, power and direction as I forge ahead into the hectic world around me. Only when I hit a wall and can't figure things out on my own, do I finally stop long enough to remember ...

John 15:4-5

Abide in Me, and I in you. As the branch cannot bear fruit of itself unless it abides in the vine, so neither can you unless you abide in Me. I am the vine, you are the branches; he who abides in Me and I in him, he bears much fruit, for apart from Me you can do nothing.

Jesus learned early on that he could do nothing without the Father's direct, daily involvement. That is why we read:

Mark 1:35

Very early in the morning, while it was still dark, Jesus got up, left the house and went off to a solitary place, where he prayed.

Luke 5:16

But Jesus often withdrew to lonely places and prayed.

He prayed all night before choosing his twelve disciples. He knew he needed to hear from His Father in order to know who to choose and why.

Why did he heal only one man at the Pool of Bethesda? Why did he wait until the storm nearly capsized the disciples boat before walking on the Sea out to them? Why did he choose the twelve disciples he chose out of all the capable men in the area?

He asked the Father to show him. He walked in constant communion with his Father and asked Him what His will was in every situation he encountered. Never once did he try to do it himself.

When will we learn? The Bible very plainly tells us we can do NOTHING without Him - at least nothing that is considered fruitful by God's standard. But if we ever do learn, it also tells us that our life will bear MUCH fruit. Oh, let it be, Lord.

Thirdly, the secret to hearing God's voice on a regular basis is pretty simple actually. In order to hear anyone's voice you have to be in close enough proximity to them. In addition, you have to be in an environment where you can actually hear. That can be different for different people.

Some people go to Starbucks or McDonalds in order to study or read. The background noise has a way of helping them focus on their material. Others would be completely distracted by the noise and the people and would never get anything accomplished. As a college student I would turn on my portable hair dryer (yes, I had one - a product of having long hair in the 70's), and the noise would completely drowned out the rowdiness in the dorm hallway or coming from my neighbors' rooms. It helped me concentrate. I found out later that I couldn't study at the library because it was simply too quiet. It was as if my thoughts were shouting at me while I tried to study. I had to go back to the sanctuary of my room ... with my hair dryer.

Whatever it takes, noise or complete silence, we need to get to that place so we can focus and concentrate on listening for the voice of the Father. He spoke to people in the Bible and He still speaks to us. *The question is - are we listening?*

It dawned on me not long ago that if the Bible says to "pray without ceasing" (1 Thess.5:17), and since prayer is a dialogue not a monologue - then God is ready, willing and able to converse with us "without ceasing" also. He wants to commune with us. He longs to speak with us, counsel us, lead us. Like any father, He wishes we would ask for His advice, His wisdom and His direction more often.

So, hearing God's voice takes physically getting to that place where we can concentrate and listen. We have to be intentional. Then we need to learn to settle out minds from the busyness in our lives and draw near to Him. He is always there, but we are so busy, so distracted that we can't hear His voice. That also takes an intentionality on our part in order to focus our thoughts on Him.

James 4:8

Draw near to God and He will draw near to you.

Hebrews 4:16

Therefore let us draw near with confidence to the throne of grace, so that we may receive mercy and find grace to help in time of need.

I have found that a great place to begin my time with Him is with thanksgiving. Thanking God for who He is and what He has done, is doing, and will do - is a form of worship. A thankful heart is great place from which to dialogue with our Father. This may lead you to read a Psalm or two, or listen to worship music on your computer or smart phone. You may even break out into song yourself. That is a sure sign that you have broken through the distractions that keep us from encountering Him.

Finally - a good measure of having truly been in God's presence is joy. Your heart will fill with joy as you voice your thanksgiving and praise to Him. Joy, as you may recall, is also one of the fruits of the Spirit (Gal.5).

Psalm 16:11

You will make known to me the path of life;
In Your presence is fullness of joy;
In Your right hand there are pleasures forever.

So, there you have it.

Jesus asked His disciples to follow Him and trust Him to do the rest. That is the same request He makes of us. Do we trust Him enough to leave the comfort of our way of doing things (independence) and follow someone we can't physically see? Do we even know Him well enough to make that decision?

Jesus is calling to you and me today. He calls every day. Every single morning He waits, He knocks on the door of our heart and asks us to invite Him in (See Rev. 3:20). He loves us more than we can possibly imagine and He longs to be involved in every aspect of our day.

He knows how to help us love our spouse. He knows how to help us raise our kids, prosper on the job and effectively deal with the stresses and issues we face every day.

He is the most loving, gentle, wise, caring, forgiving, engaging, kind and encouraging, person we will ever know - AND, He has all the wisdom, desire, resources and power necessary to change the things in our life that need to change and to lead us to a place of abundant joy and fulfillment in our life. Why wouldn't we want that?

I think we all would say "yes" we do want it - but we fall woefully short when it comes to actually doing what it takes to have it. We are addicted to ourselves and it is extremely difficult to choose against ourself. We wake up every morning to a world that revolves around us, and our selfish desires.

My challenge to you as an individual and as a spouse, is to start. Make the choice tomorrow morning to make your relationship with Christ your #1 priority. Get alone with Him, read His Word, thank Him for your blessings and ask Him to lead you. Then the next day - do it again, and again, and again.

Want to know what will happen next?

Chapter Eight
The Abundant Blessing

God very plainly says in His Word:

John 13:17

If you know these things, you are blessed if you do them.

What He doesn't say is - if you know these things, you will do them - or you will be blessed if you know these things and learn more things - or study them in small groups, or memorize these things.....

The blessing comes from "doing" them. The disciples of Jesus would never have experienced what they experienced if they had told Jesus "let me think about your offer and get back with you", or "I might be able to carve out an hour on Sundays for you".

Our Father has abundant, amazing blessings in store for each of us if we will simply do what He asks us to do - follow Him and do what He says. He promises to "make us" into the men/

women He desires us to be, fill our lives with adventure and blessing and make our lives count for eternity - IF - we will follow.

Here are some additional blessings promised by Jesus:

Psalm 23: 1-3

The Lord is my shepherd, I shall not want.

He makes me lie down in green pastures (provides for our needs); He leads me beside quiet waters. (rest, peace)

He restores my soul. He guides me in the paths of righteousness, For His name's sake.

Galatians 5:22-23

But the fruit of the Spirit is love, joy, peace, patience, kindness, goodness, faithfulness, gentleness, self-control;

Matthew 6:33

See first the kingdom of God, and all these things will be added unto you

Philippians 4:19

And my God will supply all your needs according to His riches in glory in Christ Jesus.

Could your marriage use some love, joy, peace, patience, kindness, goodness, faithfulness, gentleness or self-control? Could your personal life use for peace, restoration or guidance?

Of course - is the honest answer. So, why are we so reluctant or apathetic about running to God and falling at His feet? Why do we not hurry to His side and embrace the abundance He offers us?

All I can come up with is this - we either a) don't know we can, b) have believed the lie that we are not worthy, or c) don't care.

Hopefully (a) will never be an issue for you since you should know already that God is longing to pour out His blessing on you. Therefore, I have to go with either (b) or (c).

I am also hopeful that you have been convinced that (b) is not correct either after reading this book. No - you are not worthy and you will never be worthy of God's love and abundant blessings. That is the point.

He loves you anyway. That is called "agape" love, and it is not based on your performance, behavior or response. God loves you - period. *Remember*, there is nothing you can do to make Him love you any more than He already does, and there is nothing you can do to make Him love you less. No sin, no crime, no mistakes, no behavior, no lifestyle - nothing. You are completely and unconditionally loved.

So, shall we conclude that (c) is the correct answer for most of us then? But, how could we possibly not care about being blessed beyond our wildest imaginations?

My conclusion is this - I think we simply don't trust God. We have believed a very subtle lie that God will somehow screw up our life. Even though many of us aren't really enjoying the life we would like, we have a subconscious fear that God will strip away what little enjoyment we do have, make us give up anything we consider "fun", and ship us off to some gosh-awful, poverty stricken land to be missionaries.

We have exchanged the truth of our Father's lavish love for a lie from our mortal enemy. We have embraced religion, instead of a relationship. Principles instead of a Person. Like Adam and Eve, Satan has convinced us that God doesn't really have our best interest at heart and is going to take away our ability to live life on our own terms - and therefore - we will be miserable.

As usual, the complete opposite is the truth. No one loves us more than God and no one always has our best interest at heart. And no one desires more for us to enjoy life to the fullest. What we have to come to grips with is - our Father actually knows what will fulfill us and thrill us more than anyone else in the world - even ourselves.

You may not have ever been so foolish, but when I was in junior high (middle) school, I prayed that God would allow me to marry a little girl I was smitten with at the time. Surely no other woman (girl) would be more perfectly suited for me than this little beauty.

She was the desire of my heart. I was convinced she was all I would ever need in a wife. And, I was 13.

Thank God, He knew better. He knew that He had created someone else specifically for me, who would be exactly what I needed. And may I say - I am so glad He did, and so glad He didn't answer my adolescent prayer. We just celebrated forty years together as I write this.

God knows you better than you know yourself. What we have lost sight of - is God's goodness. We have to come to the place where we trust His heart once again - or maybe for the very first time. We have to decide that He loves us completely and knows better what we need than we do ourselves. He created us, breathed His life into us and knows exactly what we need to be completely happy and fulfilled in this short life.

But, once again, we get to choose. Every day of our lives we get to decide whether to give God the keys, or to drive ourselves. Let Him lead and we follow - or take the lead ourself and leave God in our dust.

I am also convinced that we are created with a hunger deep in our soul to walk with our Creator, Father - and until we experience that communion, we will seek fulfillment in a multitude of counterfeit alternatives offered by the world around us.

God shouts to each of us -

• I will supply all your needs according to My riches in glory. Phil. 4:19

• I have come that you might have life and have it abundantly. John 10:10

• I am the vine, you are the branches; if you abide in Me and I in you, you will bear much fruit. John 15:5

• But the fruit of the Spirit is love, joy, peace, patience, kindness, goodness, faithfulness, gentleness, self-control. Galatians 5:22-23

• Now to Him who is able to do far more abundantly beyond all that you ask or think, according to the power that works within you. Eph. 3:20

Don't you really want your life to be rich with blessing, and fruit, and fulfillment?

Don't you want your marriage to be filled with joy, and blessing, and fulfillment?

Of course you do. I do too.

God does too.

God promises abundance. He promises a life full of fruit and fruit that will remain after you are gone. A life that will mean something - to your children, your grandchildren, and their grandchildren. A life that will bring light into an ever-darkening world and a life and marriage that will bring Him glory.

He doesn't, however, promise a life of ease. Loving "like Christ" leads to a cross. That cross is what Jesus' alluded to when He said "**take up your cross, and follow me**". Loving your spouse, like Christ loves, is impossible. That is entirely the point. We cannot do it.

Compared to eternity, our life on planet Earth is a vapor, a snap of the fingers, a moment in time. Our marriage is a brief opportunity given to us by a loving Father in order for us to accomplish a mission - together.

Your life matters. Your marriage matters.

The only way we will ever understand the true purpose of each, is to voluntarily allow God to take the lead while we hang on to His robe, trusting where He is going - and finally experience the life we were created for.

Conclusions

Was this really a marriage book?

After forty years of marriage and many years of marriage mentoring, counseling and interacting with married couples in all walks of life, my answer is - YES.

The #1 enemy of your marriage – is you.

Like me, you wake up every morning of your life with a natural (after the fall) inclination toward self-seeking. We subconsciously expect the world around us, and the people around us, to conduct their business with us in mind. We have expectations (mostly unspoken) that our goals, agendas, "deserve-its", ideas, preferences and ways of doing things - are the "right" ones.

We are all addicts. We are addicted to ourselves.

What honestly needs to change is our heart. Our spouse can't do that for us and God won't do it for us. All the books, sermons, small group studies and seminars won't do a bit of good until we make the courageous decision that we need rehab.

To make matters much, much worse - the only One who has the power to change our calloused, selfish heart may be resisting doing so. What?

The Lord will tear down the house of the proud –
Proverbs 15:25

The Lord detests all the proud of heart. Be sure of this: They will not go unpunished. – Proverbs 16:5

God opposes the proud, but gives grace to the humble
– 1 Peter 5:5

Proud people say "I can do it myself". Adam and Eve's sin was "I can do it myself". Our great sin is "I can do it myself". When we declare our independence from God, He has no choice but to allow us to go our own way. Like the parent who watches a rebellious child leave home. His love isn't diminished but his heart is broken into pieces. He knows the road ahead is going to be incredibly difficult and painful.

When the strung-out, rebellious child calls home asking for money, a loving parent knows that what he/she will use it for is not good and will only prolong their rebellion - so, out of love, they say "no". They must "oppose" their own child even though it breaks their heart.

The last thing you want for your marriage is having God oppose you. Marriage was created by God and was never intended to be lived without His involvement. If we will simply allow Him to help us, lead us and empower us - we will have a 100% chance of enjoying an extraordinary marriage. Once again, the choice is ours.

The hard part is - we can make this choice today and enjoy real breakthroughs in our marriage - but then tomorrow comes. We get to decide whether to make the same choice all over again.

Like a dieter choosing to eat healthy or an alcoholic choosing not to go near a drink - we must choose every single day whether to follow a loving God who only has our best in mind - or default to our self-seeking, sinful, destructive mindset.

That is where the dying comes in.

A marriage worth dying for is the marriage we have always wanted.

It is a marriage filled with life, fruit and blessing. It is a marriage empowered and directed by God Himself.

I will remind you that this kind of marriage will not happen by simply going to church or trying to be a nice person. It will not happen magically by reading great books on marriage or attending powerful and informative seminars.

This marriage, this life, will only come when we decide to answer the invitation of the Author of marriage. I'm not talking about a one-time decision to become a Christ-follower/believer. I am talking about:

the decision to: "come follow me";

the decision to "deny yourself, take up your cross and follow me";

the decision to "open the door of our heart"

and commune with Jesus. To die to our selfishness, to fight against the gravity of self-focus - and follow. This is a deliberate, daily decision that no one else can make for us.

If we want it bad enough - we will do what it takes. If we don't, we won't. It truly is that simple. If you want an amazing, fulfilling marriage bad enough, you will find a way, you will find the time - you will.

You can whine, you can read more, attend more, study more, even pray more - but if you don't act, if you don't die - your marriage will not ever be what you want.

Even though that is a hard truth, it is the truth my wife and I share over and over again with couples, even Christian couples, who come to us with their marriages in trouble. We recommend Scripture, books, dvds as resources, but those who do not decide to DO what they are learning - fail to achieve the breakthroughs and life change they so desperately seek.

John 12:24

Truly, truly, I say to you, unless a grain of
wheat falls into the earth and dies, it remains alone;
but if it dies, it bears much fruit.

I know if you are reading this book, that your heart's desire is to have a fruitful, joyful, fulfilling marriage. There are great books that teach wonderful marriage principles and contain amazing truths and advice.

What breaks my heart is that those truths, principles and advice will mean nothing and produce nothing in your life - unless you are willing to die. Until we learn what it is to "deny ourselves" (die to selfishness), "take up our cross" (lay our lives down in sacrificial love for our spouse), and follow (not lead) Christ every single day - we will experience the ongoing frustration, anxiety and unfulfillment of a self-focused relationship.

I don't know what else to say.

I don't know how else to say it.

This truly is the bottom line.

As believers, we should never settle for an "okay" marriage.

Our marriage should be the most fulfilling adventure of all. Our neighbors, friends and family should look at our relationship and see something special. They should see a picture of Christ's love (agape) for His bride. They should see something attractive, something compelling, something they want for themselves. They should witness the uncommon, the counter-cultural, the unique.

They should see the life of God flowing through you as individuals and as a couple. They won't ever see perfection - but that is what will be compelling. They will want to know how you do it - and you will have the opportunity to tell them … .

We died. What you see in us is a direct result of His life in us and not of our own effort.

Now - we're beginning to experience a little of what God intended when He created marriage …

_____

Don't take my word for it - take God's.

It is in our dying that we find abundant life in our marriage:

> For whoever wants to save their life will lose it,
> but whoever loses their life for me will save it.
> Luke 9:24

> Truly, truly, I say to you, unless a grain of
> wheat falls into the earth and dies, it remains
> alone; but if it dies, it bears much fruit.
> John 12:24

> for me, to live is Christ and to die is gain.
> Philippians 1:21

All of us have stood before God, a minister, our spouse-to-be, our family and friends and sworn an oath. We made a covenant with our future spouse that we would *"love, honor and serve"* them *"in sickness and in health", "in good times and bad, richer and poorer" - "as long as we live - so, help us God".*

For many, those words were simply a necessary part of the wedding ceremony and repeated with good intentions. We all meant well but did we feel the weight of a commitment that may cost us something … or cost us everything? I sure didn't.

God is a covenant-making, covenant-keeping God. We have to look no farther that Malachi, Chapter 2 to see very clearly that God takes marriage and marriage vows very seriously. He created marriage for His glory and He knows what it takes from a man and a woman to not only survive, but to thrive together over decades of good times and bad - and still bear "much fruit", and for that fruit to "remain" as a praise and testimony to Him for generations. (John 12:24)

A great marriage takes dying. A God-glorifying relationship won't happen without it.

Is your marriage worth dying for?

God says it is.

The True Story of Bob Berry

Told by his former pastor - Bill Elliff

In the mid-80's I was pastoring in Norman Oklahoma. Bill Beery was a member of our church, but came only on Christmas and Easter. He was a big man (6'6") and a mechanic. In September, he was turning a wrench and his hand slipped off and he realized he was losing his grip. After a series of tests, he discovered he had Lou Gehrig's disease, ALS, and the doctors told him he would not live to see his 36th birthday, which was the following March.

In the first few weeks, two of our men went to his trailer and confronted him about whether or not he was really a Christian and led him to Christ. And Bill was gloriously saved. He continued to spiral downward physically, however. The church took up money and sent him to M.D. Anderson to see if there was any hope of recovery and after many tests they sent him home to die.

But Bill decided he would live for Christ every day that he had. He began to read his Bible. When his arms quit working, we built him a stand and he would take a pencil in his mouth and turn the pages with the eraser. In this way, he read the Bible 3-4 times a year for the final four years of his life!

When he could not longer read, we got him the Bible on tape. But the most marvelous thing was, Bill learned how to pray. He became one of the greatest intercessors I have ever known. When he prayed, God answered! He became a mighty man of prayer. I would often go to his bedside just to enlist his prayers for things that were beyond our reach.

The Thanksgiving before he died, I asked his wife to let Bill dictate to her a Thanksgiving testimony, because he was one of the happiest, most thankful men I knew! And here was part of his testimony that we shared with the church (and the secret to his great contentment and incredible fruitfulness for Christ):

"In the first few weeks after my diagnosis, I knew I was no longer in control of my life. I knew that if I was going to survive, God had to have TOTAL CONTROL. I gave him total control and from that day till this, nothing has ever been the same!"

Bill settled the issue of why he lived and found contentment and joy and purpose even though he didn't have the use of his body. Lying in a hospital bed, he continued to be a great force for the kingdom and a blessing to all who knew him. Hundreds and hundreds of lives were touched by Bill Beery. Like Paul his "earnest expectation and hope," was "that I will not be put to shame in anything, but that with all boldness, Christ will even now, as always, be exalted in my body, whether by life or by death. For to me, to live is Christ and to die is gain" (Philippians 1:20-21)

And at his funeral, four miraculous, fruitful years later, 15 adult men gave their lives to Christ!

~ Bill Elliff - Senior Pastor at The Summit Church, Maumelle, Arkansas

If we are going to get anything out of this book.....if we're going to finally enjoy the marriage we have always wanted....we have to come to the same place in our heart that Bill did. He came to realize that - "if I was going to survive, God had to have TOTAL CONTROL. I gave him total control and from that day till this, nothing has ever been the same!"

My contention is this - if we will also come to the realization that in order to have the marriage God desires us to have and we desire to enjoy, we need to "die" or as Bob put it - "give God total control" of every aspect of our lives. When we do, we will also find that "nothing will ever be the same".

If you desire to know more about how to do this - here are some practical applications for your consideration:

Applications

How do you literally apply (or "do") the things you have just read about? I have read dozens of great books, full of meaningful, Biblical truth, and yet failed miserably at applying those truths in my daily life.

The truths contained in God's Word and those selected herein are all the truths necessary for any husband/wife/marriage to be 100% successful. ***The problem is not knowing them - it is doing them.***

Going to weight loss seminars and reading great books on weight loss, nutrition and diet will provide you with facts (truth) about calories, carbs, exercise, diets, etc. - but they won't do anything at all to make pounds come off your body. It is not the knowledge, but what we "do" with that knowledge that changes things.

That said - I would like to provide some guidance regarding how to "do" what we been talking about. My prayer is that you will earnestly pray for God's help to implement (do) these things - regardless of how you feel, regardless of whether your spouse does them or not, and regardless of any results (or lack thereof) you begin to see ... just do them because God says so - and if you do them He promises to bless you. That should be motivation enough.

Prayer

Prayer is simply talking with God. God tells us to "pray without ceasing" in I Thessalonians 5:17. If prayer is a dialogue and not a monologue - then God must also be willing to talk with you "without ceasing", or anytime, any place, in every circumstance, regarding things small or large, 24/7/365.

Prayer is not about having a "prayer time" or "quiet time" or saying a prayer at a meal. Prayer, in God's mind, is a way to keep the communication channel open with you all the time. Doesn't that sound familiar? That is the relationship Adam had with God and the one we were all created to enjoy.

So, pray. Why not stop and pray now? Ask Him to help you do this. Ask Him to help you become the best husband/wife on the planet. Ask Him to help you become a deliberate spouse every single day.

There is never a valid excuse for not praying. You have time. You have place. You have reason. You may not have desire - but that is something to pray about.

Your daily "Do list" should have "Pray" at the very top of it. Every day - from here on out. This is not a quick prayer on the way to the office or an item you check off first thing and never do again. Remember the dieting analogy? Successful dieters are people who have succesfully changed their lifestyle. Every day, at least three times a days, they have to make choices regarding the foods they will eat. The serious ones make good choices and succeed - the others fail, time and time again - not because they don't want to lose weight - but because they fail the "daily choices" test.

Prayer needs to become a lifestyle. We all need to become like Jesus, who said he could do "nothing" without hearing from his Father. He arose "a great while before day" to pray, he often slipped away from the crowds and even from his disciples to pray. He stayed up all night long to pray before choosing his disciples. He was desperate to hear from God. He needed to know what to do, who to heal, what to say, etc … and so do we.

So, enough talk. We need to do. If we fail at this first application, we will not succeed at the others, because we will not have the power, wisdom or desire - to do them.

How to pray?

Talk with God like you would talk with your closest friend or family member. He already knows your thoughts and your heart, so you can tell Him anything. He will not condemn you, get mad at you or reject you. He longs to spend time with you and the very best way to do that is to talk (pray) together.

If you grew up like me and had an absent dad, or a disinterested dad or even an abusive dad, you may find it hard to draw near to a being who claims to be the most loving, caring, understanding and generous Father of all. I grew up believing that God was mad at me for my past sins, and that I had to do enough "good things" for Him to accept me and to love me like He did everyone else (Jesus loves the little children …).

What I found out later (sadly much later) was that I had believed a lie. Not only is God not mad and not waiting for me to do enough things to atone for my past - He actually loves me just like I am. I don't have to do anything for Him to completely, unconditionally love and accept me. He just does. Please don't let the enemy rob you of one more moment without knowing and embracing this truth for yourself.

Because I know He loves me, I know I can share anything with Him and it won't affect our relationship one bit. I can be angry, sad, disappointed, afraid - whatever - and simply talk with my Father about it. I am completely loved and accepted. You are too!

Another key to embracing this daily communion with the Father is being willing to listen. Conversations are interactive. Both parties speak and both parties listen. Remember - prayer is a dialogue. So, you have to take time to listen, to quiet your heart (mind) and get still. That is so incredibly difficult in today's fast-paced, technology-driven, gotta-get-it-done society. That is why so very many Christians feel disconnected to God, distant from Him and unfulfilled in their relationship with Him.

Imagine a spouse who always talked but never listened, or simply listened and never spoke … that would be maddening. You too would feel disconnected, distant and unfulfilled.

So - pray. Take the time to get alone with Him, quiet your soul, and simply have an honest conversation. Remember He has much to share with you in return, so take time to listen … and keep listening throughout the day. Keep the "airways" open all day/night also. God will speak to you through other people, through events, through His Word and through your thoughts. Keep talking - and keep listening.

Read

God wrote a best-selling book. In fact, it is the best selling book of ALL time. Don't you want to know why? The Bible is the only book ever written that the Author comes with it.

He speaks to us every single time we open it and read it. The Bible is one of the primary ways God literally and personally speaks to us. It is amazing how relavant His words are to my daily life and the circumstances I face every day. Open it. Read it. Listen to it.

This also takes time. Yes, that precious commodity that everyone has and no one wants to give up. We have the time - we just have to use it. Habits are forged over time and if you want something bad enough (weight loss, get in shape, better golf game, learn a language, further your education, etc.) you WILL do whatever it takes to achieve your goal.

Simply put - if you want an amazing relationship with God, it will cost you. It will cost you time. Time to read, time to pray and time to listen. Where will this time come from? We each have 24 hours, right? Will you choose to sleep less (go to bed later or get out of bed earlier), watch less television or spend less time chronicalling your life on Facebook?

How important is it to you? That is the pivital question. If you want it bad enough - you will find a way to do it.

Follow

Assuming you're still reading and are willing to make time to engage your Father in conversation every day and let Him speak back to you through whatever means He chooses - there is one more crucial component to this growing relationship ...

As you listen to God, you will be encouraged, prompted, urged and directed to DO something. When you ask for direction - be ready and willing to move in the direction He tells you. When you ask for wisdom - be willing to follow the advice He gives you.

Many times His answers aren't the ones we are hoping for. He may say "no" to the thing you sincerely think will make you happy or fulfilled, but always remember His love and know He will never say "no" unless He has a much better and more fulfilling answer for you elsewhere.

Remember His love for you. He will never do anything contrary to that love. He always desires the very best for you and will do whatever it takes to bring about "good and not harm" to you. Jeremiah 29:11 reminds us that His plans are to "prosper us and not harm us". Romans 8:28 tells us that He "will work all things together for our good". So - be ready and be willing to do what you feel in your heart God is asking you to do. Whether an easy thing (tell your wife/kids you love and appreciate them today) or a more difficult thing (ask your wife to forgive you for your harsh words and tone).

Nothing pleases God more than children who follow His instructions. He is ready to lavish His blessings upon us when we do what He asks. You will see. You will find walking with God in this way is much more fulfilling (and fun) than walking independently of His presence.

Marriage

So, what about my marriage?

The simple truth is this - **if** you will devote yourself to walking with the Father who loves you more than you can imagine and who can't wait to lavish His blessings upon you (by deliberately taking time to read the Bible and talk with Him throughout the day) - and **if** you will obey what He tells you to do - you will have a fantastic marriage.

Remember - marriage was never intended to be lived apart from God. Adam physically walked with God every day. Adam and

Eve physically walked with Him together. That is what we were created to experience - a life of continual communion with our Creator.

A fulfilling, God-glorifying marriage is impossible without the wisdom, power and direction of the Creator of marriage. It is only when we are walking with Him that we find the ability to love each other unconditionally.

The #1 enemy of your marriage - is you. Selfishness will choke the life out of any relationship. The more you focus on having your own needs met the more unfulfilling your relationship will become and the more miserable you will be personally.

A husband and wife focused on their walk with Christ will find that their paradigm changes and they begin to focus on meeting their spouse's needs before their own. They notice that God is enabling them to focus on their spouse and willingly serve him/her.

So, what about you? Seriously - are you walking with Christ every day? Do you deliberately set aside time to read His Word to you and to engage Him in prayer throughout your day? Are you honestly willing to do whatever He asks of you?

You can't learn your way to an awesome, fulfilling marriage. Books, dvd's, seminars are all important, but that information will not change your life or your marriage - unless you DO what it says.

It's time to stop seeking more knowledge and deliberately practice what God tells you to do in His Word. If you do, you will have a wonderful, God-glorifying relationship that will meet your deepest needs. God created marriage and He knows exactly what it takes to enjoy it to the fullest.

So - start today. Why not now? God is here. All we have to do is stop and listen, pray, and open our hearts to what He leads us to do. Here is a prayer to consider praying in order to get you heading in the right direction:

Father, thank you for creating marriage. Thank you for creating _____ (spouse) for me. Would you help me see him/ her as your divine provision and blessing for me and to treat him/her like that?

Lord, forgive me for not being more deliberate as a husband/wife and for taking _____ (spouse) for granted. Give me a more burning desire to set aside time to meet with You, to read your Word and to pray. Teach me how to calm my soul and listen to your voice. Will you also give me the desire to obey what you tell me to do, and to begin by obeying your commandment to love my spouse "as you have loved me". That means I need to learn how to give my life up for him/her and put his/her needs above my own.

I can't do that without your help. I know you love me and you want my marriage to be awesome. Help me be the very best husband/ wife I can be and to have a marriage that brings you much glory.

I trust that You will work on _____ (spouse) and that I don't need to. He/she is your child and You love them too. I know that I am only responsible for what You call me to do, so help me do it with all my heart and unto You.

Thank you Lord. I look forward to a fresh, new adventure with you - starting today.

More Resources

Keep reading great marriage books. Regularly attend marriage seminars and small groups. Never stop learning about your spouse and about marriage.

Join me every day on the following Social Media sites for more encouragement:

f Facebook: facebook.com/allinformarriage

🐦 Twitter: @husbandmentor

Website & Blog: www.allinmarriage.org

May God richly bless you as you seek Him and His plan for marriage.

Remember, be deliberate - a great marriage won't happen without it.

www.ingramcontent.com/pod-product-compliance
Lightning Source LLC
Chambersburg PA
CBHW081648270326
41933CB00018B/3395